OCCASIONAL SALMON

By

NEON REYNOLDS

Printed in Victoria, Canada

Note for Librarians: a cataloguing record for this book that includes Dewey Classification and US Library of Congress numbers is available from the National Library of Canada. The complete cataloguing record can be obtained from the National Library's online database at:
www.nlc-bnc.ca/amicus/index-e.html
ISBN 1-4120-2919-8

TRAFFORD

This book was published on-demand in cooperation with Trafford Publishing.
On-demand publishing is a unique process and service of making a book available for retail sale to the public taking advantage of on-demand manufacturing and Internet marketing. On-demand publishing includes promotions, retail sales, manufacturing, order fulfilment, accounting and collecting royalties on behalf of the author.

Suite 6E, 2333 Government St., Victoria, B.C. V8T 4P4, CANADA
Phone 250-383-6864   Toll-free 1-888-232-4444 (Canada & US)
Fax 250-383-6804   E-mail sales@trafford.com   Web site www.trafford.com
TRAFFORD PUBLISHING IS A DIVISION OF TRAFFORD HOLDINGS LTD
Trafford Catalogue #04-0747   www.trafford.com/robots/04-0747.html

13   12   11   10   9   8   7   6   5   4   3   2

CHAPTERS

In memory of

My Father

CHAPTER ONE

DEAD MENS' SHOES

Such is the pressure on good salmon fishing today that anyone wanting a rod for one or two weeks a year on a good river, with a realistic chance of catching more than the odd fish, would be well advised to start the search for his ideal slot before he reaches middle age.

Assuming that he has already discarded the idea of a timeshare – the initial cost of which is too high for so many to contemplate (although today far less than it was a few years ago) – the enthusiast must nevertheless consider all manner of things before looking for a lease that will suit him. Traps for the unwary abound and fishermen, who have perhaps never leased a rod before, need to think through carefully what really matters to them and what is of less importance.

In truth, of course, the ideal does not exist and something short of it will, inevitably, have to be accepted but there are ways of lessening the likelihood of eventual disappointment.

First, the angler should consider whether the environment in which he is going to fish is vital to him. Some will be happy casting in the shadow of a power station or surrounded by the outskirts of a town. To most this will not appeal.

Blank days, of which there will inevitably be many, are not just bearable but actually often pleasant if spent in wonderful countryside with an abundance of wildlife to look at, even if there is a marked lack of fish.

Next, how far does he want to travel? Naturally the further he is prepared to go, the more open the horizon, but a blank week 600 miles away may daunt some more than others.

Then comes the question of privacy. Does he want a beat to himself – or at least to share with one other rod – or will he take pot luck and share with five or six others? Remember that, although you may be a good mixer and think you get on well with most people and while most fishermen

1

are the gentlest and kindest of people, there are exceptions. A week spent constantly arguing about who shall fish where can be a disaster.

Does our hypothetical angler feel he would rather run the risk of finding no water in the spate river he has chosen – perhaps for several years running – or would he prefer to plump for one of the many hydro-ed salmon rivers, where a minimum amount of water is guaranteed but the rare bonanza possible on a natural stream if the water is right, can almost be discounted from the start?

Does he fish fly only? If so will he accept what others may not, and lease a rod where prawn or spinning, if not the dreaded worm, is also allowed?

Must the fish be fresh-run springers, or does he prefer more fish but less quality? This is a vital question and leads to perhaps the most important factor of all – from what part of his salmon fishing does he derive his main pleasure? From that delirious moment of the actual take? From playing the fish? From the successful landing of it? From taking it home for the freezer and the dinner table?

Alternatively, is he one of those lucky people who just love casting a fly into a near perfect pool while the fish are of secondary importance?

Does he want a gillie or does he prefer to find his own way around, make his own mistakes and thus, while wasting a lot of time initially, eventually come to that position of ultimate satisfaction where he catches fish from places that few others even try?

Does he want to wield a 14 ft pole all day or be content with a smaller river? Is deep wading a disadvantage? Should every part of the river be accessible by car or will he be prepared to walk considerable distances to reach his beat?

Must he stay in a hotel or is he happy to self cater? Or will he agree to stay in a hotel if to do so is a requirement of the lease?

Having decided on these points – I suggest allocating each point a mark out of five and starting the search by looking only at places that offer a rod on conditions in line with everything that scores an average of three or above –

there are always further ways to reduce the odds against getting the wrong fishing.

Always ask for details of the number of fish caught over the past five years, not only in your chosen week but also in each of the two weeks either side, and make sure you know how many rods have striven to achieve that figure.

Do not write off replies that say "but the river has never been seriously fished at this time of year". By doing so you may cut yourself off from a real bargain. Nevertheless, you would be unwise not to ask some pretty searching questions as to why that has happened.

If you are considering taking a beat without a gillie, always ask for a map of the water before you sign the lease. The best run fisheries will have a short guide to each beat and, if you are extremely lucky, the pools may even be numbered.

Ask for the name of someone who lives not too far away from you who has fished the water before and have a short chat with them on the telephone. No angler would refuse to divulge his real feelings to you and, if he has been going to the river in question for some seasons, he will tell you honestly what you can expect.

Never forget that fishing is a field sport. While the amount you may pay over a period of years can be expected to bear some relation to the number of fish you will catch, to pay a huge sum of money is never a guarantee of success.

*   *   *

I actually wrote the above some years ago and the fact that, since then the number of salmon returning each year to the rivers of Britain has further declined, has only exacerbated the problem. At the same time, while the cost of time shares may have been slashed, simple rents have at least held steady, while accommodation is no less expensive than it was at the end of the last century. The cost of catching each salmon has thus rocketed further and is made even less attractive by the requirement of many landlords that the fisherman should return most of his catch anyway.

Drier, warmer summers have resulted in the spate rivers offering fewer and fewer weeks of satisfactory fishing while the afforestation programme has come to fruition leading to a situation where water, when it does come, stays in the river for a shorter period.

Pressure is continually mounting and forcing more and more people to look abroad for their salmon fishing. These trips are expensive and also, in many cases, lack the "feeling" that comes with a traditional fishing holiday in this country.

In future anglers may have to compromise to an even greater extent than I have had to do over the past fifty years. I just hope that future generations may have half the fun that I have had trying to catch salmon over that period.[1]

---

[1] Reprinted by kind permission of "Trout and Salmon".

CHAPTER TWO

AFTER MY FATHER.

On the 4th September 1952 my father stood at my shoulder as I played a large, fresh run salmon in the Rock Pool on the Brae Water of the River Spey. At the age of fifteen and an almost totally inexperienced salmon fisherman, I had allowed the cast to become wrapped round the fish's head shortly after hooking it from the boat in the middle of the river and had had little control over it ever since. I was using a 10 ft single handed tubular steel rod, which, though immensely strong for its length, was not in the same class as the 18 footers generally used on this river fifty years ago and the heavy water of this famous pool allowed the salmon to do much as it liked. I battled with it for over an hour before, quietly coached by my father, I was finally able to bring it within reach of gillie Jimmy Morrison's gaff and, in a flash, it was on the bank.

Sea liced and a bar of silver it weighed 17 lbs and was to remain the largest fish I had caught for a further 43 years.

Earlier in the same week my father had landed a 27 pounder from Lower Aultdearg which was the biggest fish of his life.

* * *

A little over three months later I stood beside his bed in the London Clinic. He was little more than a skeleton, racked with pain, grimacing and fighting for breath as he went through the last hours of the agony of lung cancer.

Two days later he was dead, released from a hell that I never wish to see again and the few minutes sight of which has coloured my view about certain aspects of life and death ever since.

The effect of my father's early demise at the age of 57 was naturally disastrous for my mother and sisters as well as for me. It was not long since so many children and wives had

had their fathers and husbands swept away in the Second World War and, in itself, our position was not necessarily more dire than those of many others at that time, but when, as in my case, one has been born with only one hand, it is perhaps allowable to say that, at the age of fifteen, the loss of one's guide and mentor, who had taken so many correct decisions in my interest in that short time, was a particularly heavy burden to bear.

With his death disappeared any chance of more quality salmon fishing being available to me until or unless I could pay for it myself.

*   *   *

Frank Neon Reynolds was born on 29th July 1895 in Romsey in Hampshire. He came from a relatively well-to-do background, his father being a captain and later Commodore of the Union Castle Line, in charge of their ships plying between Southampton and Capetown in the heyday of steamship travel.

My grandfather was by all accounts a bit of a womaniser and when his third son and his twin brother, who died early in infancy, were born he was in the middle of a voyage on which one of his favourite lady passengers, Lady Nea Hamilton was on board. My grandmother was persuaded to name the surviving baby after her, the Christian name being suitably masculinised for the purpose.

This, at any rate, is the story that I tell whenever I am asked where my strange name came from, for my parents did me the utmost disservice of passing it on to me. Proud though I have been to bear my father's name, the boredom of constantly explaining the derivation of it has long since dispelled its gloss in my eyes. Oh to be a Peter or a Tom!

Frank Reynolds was determined to become a doctor and was duly sent to Epsom School which was in those days acknowledged as the best medical school in the country. Hardly had he left there and started his training at St. Thomas's than the World War began. He joined up immediately choosing to serve in the navy rather than the more popular ranks of Kitchener's army. It was not a surprising decision in view of his family background but it was one that almost certainly saved his life

Had he opted for the army he would surely have become yet another of the endless line of subalterns who became fodder for the German machine guns in the pitiful slaughter of trench warfare. As it was, however, his war, whilst far from dull, was one in which, as a sailor, he had a realistic chance of survival.

As a result of his limited medical training before the outbreak of hostilities, my father was at first sent to serve on hospital ships dealing with the blood bath of the failure at Gallipoli. From 1914 to early 1916 he acted first as a "dresser" and later as anaesthetist on board H.M.H.S. Guildford Castle, Glenart Castle and finally Letitia. It does not take great imagination to conjur up a vision of endless wounded men being swung aboard these huge white painted ships bearing a large red cross on their sides, where the medical staff would try desperately to make up for the tribulations they had suffered and give them some degree of comfort in the searing heat of the Eastern Mediterranean. Wards were overcrowded, nurses and doctors overworked and ventilation could be non existent. The high resultant mortality rate amongst even the less seriously wounded was unacceptable but unavoidable.

At the end of the Dardanelles campaign my father had gained enough experience at the sharp end of emergency operations for him to be transferred to destroyers as a Surgeon-Lieutenant with total responsibility for the health of all the crew. It was also the surgeon's job to look after the liquor on board and one of the few stories my father ever told me about his wartime service concerned this part of his job. A quantity of drink went missing. He was accused of being an accessory to this theft for his signature apparently appeared in the register as having authorised its issue. Interviewed by the Captain he was asked whether the signature in question was his and he was able to prove that he always put two dots or full stops after his name. In the register in question the forgery showed only one. To this day my own signature contains the same two full stops but luckily they have never been called upon to act as silent witnesses to my own innocence.

Frank Reynolds now joined H.M.S. Oak serving with Jellicoe's Home Fleet based at Scapa Flow. "Oak" was in the destroyer flotilla at the Battle of Jutland at the end of May 1916 and some remarkable photographs taken by my father during the battle, showing the big ships firing at the enemy over the horizon, are in the Imperial War Museum.

The destroyers were not seriously involved in the battle and no damage was done to his ship. leaving my father with time to fiddle with his camera while other ships in the fleet took the pounding that meant that Jutland could never be regarded as more than a draw.

A very different duty followed shortly afterwards. While the fleet was still licking its wounds and undergoing repairs at Scapa, Lord Kitchener travelled north to join the cruiser H.M.S. Hampshire that was to take him on his journey to Russia. My father's camera was again in use as he took the last known photograph of Kitchener alive. I still have the sepia coloured shot in its original frame, showing the Minister for War meeting Jellicoe on board his flagship, H.M.S. Iron Duke, before transferring to the cruiser. It is interesting in view of what was to follow that everyone in the picture is wearing oilskins or a waterproof of some sort.

Later the same day "Hampshire" sailed for Russia escorted by the destroyers and in dreadful weather. So bad was the storm that the smaller ships could not keep up the speed required for security reasons and, not long after leaving Scapa, they were ordered to return to harbour leaving the cruiser to continue her voyage unescorted. She was alone therefore when, later that evening, she hit a mine off the Shetlands and quickly sank, taking most of her company and Kitchener and his entire staff with her.

As soon as news of the disaster reached the Home Fleet, the destroyers were ordered out again, despite the weather, to try to rescue any survivors, although the likelihood of anyone staying alive in the maelstrom of the North Sea that day was very small. All that was found was a quantity of wreckage and "Oak" picked up a mahogany ladder later proved to have come from "Hampshire". Each of the "Oak's" officers was given a piece of this wood as a momento and my father had his made into a cigarette box which I still have today. It bears a silver mount inscribed:

"Made from the wood of H.M.S. Hampshire
sunk 6th June 1916
while conveying Lord Kitchener to Russia."

The next year my father was transferred to "Vivid" and in 1918 finally to "Broke". He took part in the second and successful raid on Ostend in May, temporarily joining H.M.S. Pembroke at Chatham for that purpose.

Insulated from the horror of the trenches by his original decision to join the navy, he was demobbed in 1919 and returned to his medical studies.

* * *

The next eleven years saw my father qualifying, specialising in obstetrics and then slowly climbing the ladder in that branch of the profession until the years of relative poverty were behind him. In 1925 he married and in 1930 he was asked by Sir Henry Simson to assist him at the Duchess of York's[1] impending "accouchement".

The baby[2] was to be born at Glamis Castle and, like so many in that era, long before the days when inducing babies to arrive on time became fashionable, was late! During the long wait the press reported that he and Sir Henry went fishing and I have a letter written by him from Glamis to my mother which states "Henry is very keen on this fishing and I like it….." from which I deduce that he had never seriously fished before.

Four years later, now undeniably at the top of his particular tree, and living with my mother and two daughters

---

[1] Later of course Queen Elizabeth and then the Queen Mother
[2] Princess Margaret

in a large house in Devonshire Place just across the road from the London Clinic, he took a beat on the best part of the Spey. Annual holidays in Scotland, fitted in alarmingly closely between his patients' babies, replaced trips to Symons Yat on the Wye and it is clear that by now he was firmly hooked on salmon fishing.

There is however proof that my father was still at this time something of a beginner. An old film showing him playing a 20 pounder in the Dipple Pool on the Spey, which I had believed long since lost, has recently reappeared as a video in the hands of my cousin in South Africa and he kindly had it copied for me. It shows the obvious concern of the gillie as the top of the huge rod almost drops into the water on several occasions. When watching the film as children we always screamed "Keep yer rod up!" and, when I saw it again for the first time more recently, my immediate reaction was that it was a pretty bad example of how to play a fish!

He must have improved quickly as for the next five years the same beat was taken, a wing of the nearby Gordon Castle rented and the Reynolds family, dogs, cars and staff entrained for the north each August.

In 1937 I was born, having been preceded by my two sisters who appeared in 1927 and 1931, and in 1939 the world was plunged again into war. This time my father's duty lay at home. The family was sent to a succession of rented cottages in Sunningdale to which he motored down from London at weekends if his work allowed. Private patients dried up and the always precarious family finances suffered. Careless of this, however, we grew up with rabbits, chickens, a pony for my younger sister, through seemingly endless summer days. Bombs, doodle bugs and badly damaged aircraft, both enemy and friendly, were never far away.

The moaning of the air raid sirens, whilst never actually frightening, were nonetheless unsettling and we knew them all by nicknames and were well aware that, when the nearest was sounded, we would have to get out of our warm beds and go down to shelter under the dining room table. As one complete side of that room consisted of glass

French windows it seemed later to have been a place of only relative safety.

By the time the war ended so had my father's prosperity. Never one for much careful consideration for the future, he found himself, with his practice severely curtailed, wishing that he had spent less in the good days and constantly concerned about the financial welfare of his family in the new world in which everyone found themselves. The National Health Service came into being, and the medical profession changed for ever.

*   *   *

Despite these problems, all of which had probably not yet manifested themselves, we made a quick trip to Scotland in 1946 to fish the Dee at Banchory. The journey was not a major success. It has always amazed me that my father, who was the best mannered, most considerate of men, had a first class sleeper, while my mother accompanied us three children in a four-berth compartment from which we all caught fleas[1]. The holiday gave me my first opportunity to cast a fly and, using an old greenheart trout rod from the end of one of a number of groynes, I duly landed my first small trout.

I have no recollection of being thrilled by this and my memories of the Dee are of the vaguest. I certainly do not think my father caught a salmon and my overriding impression is one of cold wetness so that probably the river was out of order for a lot of the time.

In 1947 Scotland was forsaken for the clearly cheaper and more easily reachable West Country and we had the first of a number of wonderful stays at the Carnarvon Arms in Dulverton. Full board was 7 guineas a week for adults, 3 guineas for children, salmon fishing was extra at £1 a day but trout fishing on the Barle and the Exe was free. Following a dreadful winter of appalling weather and fuel shortages, clothes rationing and misery, the summer of that year really

---

[1] almost certainly the compartments had been used by troops and possibly as ambulance coaches

was glorious. As I had had riding lessons at various times throughout the war years in Sunningdale, I was taken out on a pony on Exmoor – just once! It was to be the last time I rode for 30 years. Below the hotel about two fields away lay the River Barle. Slowly, sometimes with my father's help and advice and sometimes alone, I learnt to cast properly with a tiny 6ft split cane rod that I had been given for my birthday. I learnt where the trout would lie, when they were most likely to take, what flies were most likely to attract them. I learnt how important the weather was, I started to understand river lore, how currents affected the speed of the fly, how, as the height of the water changed, so would the best part of a pool or run move. When my father was behind me he was, from the beginning. most emphatic that I should "let the line come right round!" – his early training in this and so many other respects stood me in good stead later when salmon so often took "on the dangle" – a dreadful expression that I can not remember being used in those days. The usual impatience of youth generally resulted in me wishing to get the line out of the water too early in order to get the fly back into a more promising position as quickly as possible and before it was properly fished out. How many fish are never given their chance to take the fly because of this hurry?

Although he caught the odd salmon at Dulverton I never saw my father playing a fish there and, probably as a result of that, I was happy fiddling with the mainly tiny trout, often below the 7 inch limit, and the myriads of salmon parr that were only too keen to hook themselves on to anything vaguely resembling food. Slowly, however, I began to want to catch something more serious. Once my father went out with another guest at the hotel as darkness fell and cast a dry fly into the still pool above the weir. In the morning there were three or four trout of about 2 lbs on the slab in the hall that they had caught the night before. I remember that the biggest of these was far darker than normal with huge black spots along its whole length and hardly a red one to be seen. I was green with envy and begged to be allowed to go out with them the next night, but the hours after dinner were rightly reserved for my father to relax in his own way without the burden of me round his neck.

On another occasion both my parents and I were fishing below the railway bridge that carried the Taunton to Barnstaple line over the Exe. It had rained overnight and both the Barle and Little Exe which met a short way upstream, were carrying flood water off Exmoor. Unlike most lowland rivers these tributaries were quite clear even when in spate: the water came straight off the moor and, that far upstream, was never sullied by the mud and filth with which it arrived in the lower reaches. As the river level started to drop so the trout began to take. Small by many standards they might have been but inside an hour we had a dozen on the bank, mostly between half a pound and a pound. To me this was an unforgettable experience.

When things quietened down we wandered downstream to where another guest was fishing the Bend Pool for salmon. I can remember his name to this day but will not quote it. Suffice to say that he was a brash, loud mouthed man, anathema to my parents. It was the rule that the first salmon caught belonged to the guest, the second to the hotel and so on. We saw one fish lying on the bank and asked him if he had had any more. He had hardly finished replying that this was his only bit of success when I saw the tail of another one poking out from under a sweater on the grass. Unthinking and with the carelessness of youth, I pulled the jersey aside exclaiming that he must have forgotten the second one. The pleasure my parents derived from this unmasking of "loudmouth's" dishonesty was out of all proportion to his crime, about which he was thick skinned enough to show little embarrassment.

In 1948 and 1949 we went both to Dulverton in the spring and to Scotland and Wales respectively in the summer. The Scottish trip was interesting in that the fishing was entirely on the lochs attached to the Scourie Hotel in the far north of Sutherland. I remember that we travelled overnight to Lairg with my mother's Wolseley in a van of its own attached to the back of the train. On arrival at Lairg a tiny tank engine, a bit like Thomas, fussed around and duly delivered

13

the car back to the bay platform almost before we had disembarked from the sleeper.

At Scourie I caught my first sea trout of about ½ pound and numerous small brownies . The only real success came when my parents went off to fish Loch Stack, courtesy of the Duke of Westminster whose wife was a patient of my father's. It was a stormy day and I was frightened that they might have drowned when dinner time came and they had not returned. Of course all was well and eventually they came in with half a dozen of the most beautiful sea trout between three and seven pounds. What a day that must have been. It was at a time when Loch Stack was still prolific in the extreme and long, long before, in common with all the west coast of Scotland, it suffered so dreadfully from the almost total disappearance of these lovely fish.

Wales was a disaster. It rained almost incessantly. The hotel at Maentwrog was perfectly awful and I cannot remember the river at all. I do recollect that there was another family there called Ransom, the son John being at Eton, for where I was hopefully destined. He was railway mad and spent his time walking along the track of the Ffestiniog line that was just starting to be restored. Day after day he came in and had to empty the water out of the pockets of his mackintosh. So much for Wales!

During our last holiday at the Carnarvon Arms another dimension was added to our fishing. Careless of the financial angle, it was my father's habit to accept presents from grateful patients or their husbands, often in lieu of a fee. He had recently looked after Lady Eldon and his lordship owned a stretch of the Exe further downstream at Cove just above Tiverton. It was arranged that we should have a couple of days on his beat. This to me was a revelation. Here the Exe was bigger and stronger, it was not overfished as was the hotel water at Dulverton, and it held bigger trout and more salmon. The beat was divided roughly in half by another railway bridge which carried the Exe Valley Line from Exeter to Dulverton. Up here at infrequent intervals chugged the two coaches of the train that served the small towns and villages along the line of the river, pushed or pulled by another diminutive tank engine. One had to walk across the bridge to get from the lower part of the beat to the upper and I was always terrified that the train would come at the exact moment when we were in the middle of it. In reality it was the labrador, Spey, who was most at risk all day and my father insisted that he should never wear a collar on the riverbank because he had heard dreadful tales of dogs getting their collars caught in the rails and being killed.

A hundred yards above this bridge there was a delightful run, a classic trout holding stretch. You had to get into the water from the right bank near the head of the run, wade out and fish down beneath the trees. In the centre of the river these were high enough not to interfere with one's casting and being left handed and with my 6 ft rod I had no trouble in clearing them. Three quarters of the way down this run I hooked the biggest trout with which I had ever made contact. In response to my cries for help my father appeared from nowhere, waded quietly into he water behind me, prevented me from playing it too hard or too hurriedly, and finally slipped the net under it. It weighed a pound and a half and, strangely, remained the largest trout I had caught until I landed a two and a half pound cannibal on the Farrar thirty four years later.

At Cove I also saw both my parents hook, play and land a salmon for the first time. Denscombe was not so much a gillie as Lord Eldon's water bailiff, and he had been sent down to show us the pools and lies and generally acquaint us with the beat. He showed my mother a long glide with a narrow neck at the top, a shallow slope of shingle on the near side and a high bank opposite. It was clear that the deep water lay close to the far bank. "Now you fish down Denscombe's Stream" my mother was adjured, "Keep the fly within a foot or so of the far bank and let it come right round. You'll get a fish there, ma'am and, when you hook it, I'll come back and land it for you!"

Salmon fishing was clearly very easy. My mother was a skilled fisher in her own right, having been taught by the Spey gillies before the war, and she duly fished quietly down the run landing her fly, cast after cast, metronomically a foot to eighteen inches from the far bank. The fish took about halfway down, the reel screamed and unhurriedly and without fuss my mother played it. After about five minutes it was just beginning to tire when Denscombe duly appeared, but to my consternation he was carrying neither net nor gaff. This did not concern him in the least. "Just play it dead" he told my mother in his soft West Country burr "and I'll do the rest". Shortly the fish of about 8 lbs was lying on its side in the water and Denscombe reached into his pocket and brought out a handkerchief. "Now draw it slowly towards the bank" he instructed and my mother obeyed. As its head touched the shingle Denscombe came quietly up behind it, reached down with his handkerchief over his hand, grasped the fish by the wrist of the tail and, rather than lifting it out of the river, propelled it up the shingle beach to safety.

I had learned another lesson. For many years I used a gaff to land my fish but when, eventually, catch and release came on the scene and nets and tailers replaced those awful instruments, I always reached for my handkerchief!

Later that evening, when Denscombe had disappeared for his "tea", my father fished the bottommost pool on the beat which ran under a road bridge. A passer-by had seen a fish jump there earlier and he made a short detour to tell us and then, somewhat to my father's irritation, stationed himself on the bridge to watch as he fished the pool down. He called out that he could see the fly perfectly and a couple of casts later yelled out "You've got him" fractions of a second before the rod bent and the reel sang.

That evening my parents' two salmon and my trout took pride of place on the slab back at the Carnarvon Arms.

*   *   *

That was 1949 and I was 12. These days one sees photographs of children aged four or five proudly holding their first salmon and I often wonder how much help they received to land them, but fifty years ago 12 was quite young enough to get hooked on such an expensive sport. In fact I had to wait a further year before I caught my first "fish" and again it was thanks to a grateful patient that I got the chance.

The Earl of Antrim then owned the whole of the Glenarm River in Co. Antrim, Northern Ireland and arrangements were made for us to fish it as his guests in the summer of 1950. We crossed from Stranraer to Larne on a violent, stormy day in August on board the virtually new car ferry, M.V. Princess Victoria. She was one of the earliest drive on/drive off ferries although she had vehicle gates only at the stern. I have never been anything other than a bad and frightened sailor and was more than glad when we reached the haven of Lough Larne which provided some shelter from the gale force winds.

Not very long afterwards the same ferry sank with appalling loss of life on the same crossing when the seas battered down her inadequate stern doors in the middle of the angry Irish Sea.

Arrived safely however, we drove the few miles north up the coast to the small village of Glenarm, where we stayed at the only hotel, which was in fact little more than a pub. It was, however, a pub whose friendliness and warm welcome was most genuine and was backed up by a week of food the like of which we, from the still ration bound Great Britain, had not seen since before the war. I can remember little enough about the village except that it was somewhat dreary, consisting of nothing more than the single main road with a bridge over the river in the middle of it. The weather was certainly bad because my parents both caught plenty of fish for which, on that short spate stream, rain was essential.

During one flood, when the river rushed brown under the bridge, we did not fish that day and instead, in the early evening, we went out in the bay with one of the local fishermen and caught huge quantities of mackerel. So stormy had it been that a shoal of these fish had been driven right into the harbour. As darkness fell we found ourselves in one of a dozen boats, rowing round and round in a tight circle below the harbour walls, trailing lines with feathered hooks on them just a few feet behind the boat, and hauling them in with four, five or six gleaming mackerel on them each time.

As I had come to Glenarm still only armed with my 6 ft trout rod, I assume that any requests I had made to start fishing for salmon following the exploits at Cove had been turned down but, in that strange way that life has of taking matters into its own hands, the river had other ideas. The water being high for most of the week, the grilse running in shoals and the trout flies I was using being necessarily larger than usual, it was inevitable that at some point I should meet a salmon. I duly did so in the middle of a lovely, classic pool with a narrow throat broadening in a wide deep run. The fish took in the middle of the stream and both my parents were present. I have no idea of its size for we never saw it. It cruised once or twice up and down the middle of the stream, unconcerned by the minimal pressure I was able to exert with my tiny rod and then came to rest. Of course I know now that it must have got itself round a rock or a submerged branch of some sort. We tried everything, pulling from downstream, upstream, the side, letting the line go slack, hurling rocks at it but no movement of any sort resulted. Finally we just pulled and my light trout cast broke as easily as one would expect.

If I do not recollect being heart broken or even dramatically upset, it was certainly because my father now took the hint, tied on a proper salmon cast for me and the deed was done. Now I was a salmon fisherman. Nor did I have to wait long for my first success. Next day we were on the top beat where the river naturally became even smaller. I walked alone upstream to investigate the head of the beat and found a small round pool with a low waterfall at the top and a pronounced lip at the bottom. It demanded only a few casts and I could reach the far side quite easily. In the way that grilse do in small pools, the fish emerged from the depths and took my size 4 Akroyd with a bang. It was not a big fish and it could not get out of the pool but I nevertheless had a problem. The banks were high, I was alone, I had neither net nor gaff and in any case needed all my virtually non existent skill and total concentration to play the fish. There was nothing for it but to yell!

If one is standing beside a fast flowing river the sound of one's own voice seems drowned by the noise of the stream and one imagines that nobody can possibly hear one from more than a short distance away. This is not true. A cry reverberates and echoes and can often be picked up a few hundred yards off. I did not know this and, as the small grilse started to tire of pulling my line round and round the pool, I began to wonder what to do next. The only answer seemed to be to shout louder. My relief when my father arrived, gaff in hand, was only matched by my irritation at his apparent total lack of urgency! (He was the same when walking the dog in the park in London – if it took off and proceeded to rape some tasty bitch 200 yards away, he would amble over, with apparent total unconcern, to sort things out!) Almost immediately the fish was on the bank. It was a rather red 7 lb grilse in moderate condition.

However, it was my first salmon. Had I known what pleasure salmon fishing would hold for me in the future, my feelings of exhilaration and satisfaction at that moment would have been even more overwhelming. Had I known how long it would take me to catch so few more in the future, I might have given up there and then.

When we joined the ferry for Stranraer a couple of days later a nephew of Lord Antrim's, slightly older than myself was on board. He too had had a fish out of the Carrie Pool. At that height of water, late in the season, it was clearly a "certain cast". I always in future fished any similar likely looking small pots or holes of water – it was another lesson well learned.

Although it was well before the recent troubles in Ireland started, it was to be a further nine years before I returned to that wonderful but sad country.

*   *   *

1951 was to be a blank year for me. As character training went it was excellent, but in every other way my fishing was to be a disaster.

Once again grateful patients were tapped for our holiday and once again we returned to Scotland. My father had recently operated on the Duke of Atholl's mother and his grace offered him a weeks fishing on the Tilt, a small spate river on the Tay system which joins the Garry at Blair Atholl. As in these days one seems constantly to fish spate rivers at times of drought and to go to cricket matches on days of pouring rain, so in one's youth cricket days were endlessly hot and spate rivers permanently full of water. Certainly Glen Tilt had no shortage of rain that year and once again we were faced with a river which was full of fish: but this time I was fishing for them from the start. I had been given a single handed 10 ft tubular steel rod. Long before the days of glass fibre this was the only alternative to split cane or greenheart and, foot for foot, steel was far stronger. It had a rather stiff feel to it which, while enabling me to cast long distances, did not lead to lying the line on the water terribly straight or very softly. Neither of these disadvantages proved to matter much. I used the rod for all my salmon fishing until it finally broke in 1978, twenty seven years later. To go with the rod was a gun metal reel by Malloch of Perth. Doubtless it was top of the range at the time for my father never did things by halves, but as value for money goes it was unbeatable – I used it from that day until the rim finally gave way on the Farrar last summer, fifty-one years later. I was so attached to this reel that, on our way south that year we made a short detour off the main A9, drove through the village of Blair Atholl and I gave it a decent burial by throwing it into the Tilt, where I had first used it, from the old road bridge.

Neither rod nor reel was to be much help to me that year however, for I was about to suffer one of those incredible runs of bad luck, the reasons for which are indiscernible, and about which nothing can be done. While my parents caught fish all round me, I hooked and lost six in a row. I can remember only two. With the river high and heavy, a large fish took me just yards above the lip at the tail of a pool under the near bank. I cannot believe that, even with the experience that I have today, I would have held on to it – at that stage I had no idea what to do and did nothing. In fact that might have been correct but the fish disappeared over the lip and was gone in a flash. The final occasion on which I made contact that week was when, with my father beside me, I hooked a small grilse – it may even have been a sea trout – and he encouraged me, after all my previous disasters, to just play it quietly and gently and make sure of landing it. When it came off I burst into tears.

The whole of that week was an unhappy one. Once I was dragged from the river to join the beaters on the moor driving grouse towards the butts. The moor was easy – the hillsides of shale were sheer hell. I was shy and uneasy in the company of young people, of whom there a number around, who knew far more about the countryside than I did and took shooting in their stride, while to me it was uncharted territory. We had to go to dinner at Blair Castle in dinner jackets and afterwards we played "The Game" which was all the rage at the time. I was asked to act out "Honesty is the Best Policy". I have always thought that it would have defeated many better men than me. It was a hateful evening but, when we stop nowadays at the House of Bruar on our way north, it is rather amusing to remember that I once dined at Blair Castle as a guest of the Duke.

Though I had doubtless learned a few worthwhile lessons, this holiday had not furthered my angling education a great deal and another twelve months lay ahead before I would get another chance.

*   *   *

I have never discovered whether my father had any idea at the start of 1952 that he was desperately ill, but it has always seemed likely that he was determined to go back to the Spey once more before he died. The family fortunes were at a low ebb, the house in Devonshire Place had been sold (for £3,000!) and we were living in Harley House, a block of dark and gloomy flats on Marylebone Road, while my father had a consulting room at the top of Harley Street itself.

Whatever the reason may have been, a family party was made up consisting of my parents and me, my mother's cousin Gerry Lycett-Green, to whom my father often found it hard to be civil, and her two children by a former marriage, Jock and Julia Williamson. Julia later found some notoriety as a very beautiful deb and went on to be a much married woman who, I fear, may never have found much happiness despite her looks.

To this mixed bunch was added Ian Bailey. Ian was one of my parents' closest friends and had made a fortune out of glass. He had fished the Spey regularly with my father before the war and was, in the nicest possible way, as flashy as my father was down to earth.

There were no longer any wings of Gordon Castle to stay at and we took over most of the Spey Bay Hotel, five miles from Fochabers at the mouth of the river. It was bleak and I remember very little more about it except that when turning our Humber Super Snipe round in the forecourt I got it in forward instead of reverse gear and nearly killed our beloved labrador "Spey". The hotel probably had very little going for it.

Although I still have a water stained list of the thirteen fish that my parents and I caught in that fortnight, I can only recollect the details of my own three and one of my father's. Our fishing ran from the top of the Rock Pool to the bottom of Lower Aultdearg and was divided somewhere in the middle so that each part of our party fished a different bit of the river every other day. The two gillies were responsible for their own two halves of the water. Jimmy Morrison, who looked after the guests on the Rock, was a typically dour Scot who seemed to me at my tender age to be as old as time. I heard recently, however, that he had only finally retired in 1980 so he cannot have then been more than about 40. At the lower end of the water we were in the hands of Jock Burgess, a completely different character, outgoing, amusing and enthusiastic. Both had been on the river before the war and were therefore well known to my parents whom they welcomed, if not literally with open arms, at least with genuine pleasure.

Those readers who know the Spey today would not have recognised it then. The Rock itself was of more uniform depth the whole way across, making wading impossible even within a few feet of either bank, while the huge conifers that now stand close to the left hand bank were mere saplings. The

Ewe Pool did not exist and the Rock ran straight into Lord March's Pool. At the bottom of this was Lord Algernon's which only fished from the far side, followed by Otter's Cave under the huge red sandstone cliff and finally Lower Aultdearg. We probably fished three rods on the Rock and three on the rest of the beat.

Today, I understand, the Rock is a mere shadow of its' former self but in 1952 it was a most prolific pool. Even assuming that we were fishing two rods between us out of the total of six available and that the two remaining pairs of rods also landed thirteen fish per pair, the total of 39 for the fortnight was moderate in the extreme. More than half of these would have come from the Rock. Lord Algernon's, which proved a virtually certain cast each morning, would have accounted for most of the rest, leaving only the odd fish for the rest of the lower beat.

On the second afternoon my father landed the biggest salmon he ever caught. He was fishing the quite small and confined Lower Aultdearg Pool with our chauffeur, Butcher, acting as his gillie. Butcher naturally normally wore a smart uniform and peaked cap in London but on holiday this was changed for a brown trilby and tweeds in which he somehow never looked quite at home. I was very fond of him, and I believe he of me and I was sad in the extreme when he later behaved rather badly after my father's death and made things unnecessarily difficult for my mother, who had more than enough on her plate at the time.

Perhaps it was lucky that the big fish was rather stale. Like a lot of old red cocks it moved sedately and inexorably round the pool for about a quarter of an hour before we saw it and it then quickly surrendered. Butcher was handed the rod while my father gaffed it. There was no particular elation over its size, probably in part because it was so stale, but also I suspect because my father was even then feeling severely below par.

Next morning it was my turn to go first down Lord Algernon's Pool. On the first day my mother had had a small fish out of it and another rod had taken a second on the following morning. A pattern was already being set – a taking fish would move into the lie overnight and the first person down the pool would, virtually every day, hook it. I was taken across the tail of Lord March's in the boat and Jock duly set me in at the top of the run before returning to the left bank to look after his other guests.

He was soon back. In the usual place I hooked the overnight arrival. My records show that I was fishing a No.4 Hairy Mary and that it took me 12 minutes to land the fish. It was clean and beautiful and even before receiving, probably with a marked teenage lack of grace, the plaudits of Jock Burgess, my father and Ian Bailey, who were watching from the other bank, on the way I had played it, I knew that I had actually done so rather well.

Having broken my duck on the Spey and landed my first salmon really worthy of the name, which was closely followed by the big fish from the Rock described at the beginning of this chapter, I felt that the sky was the limit. As so often with people coming fresh into any sport it all looked suddenly very easy. Perhaps luckily, this turned out not to be the case for, during the rest of the fortnight I touched only one more fish, which was duly safely landed. Below Lord Algernon's Pool the river made a sharp turn to the left and flattened out into a wide slower pool known as Otter's Cave. Again a boat was used to reach the best part of it and as I fished down it a salmon jumped well below me.

Jock Burgess announced that we would "have that one!" and twenty minutes later what he described as a perfect greased line rise just where the fish had shown before, resulted in it being just as perfectly hooked. It was my first and unbelievably my last experience of being able to see the full length of my line on the almost oily water, to see the splash of the fish taking virtually on the surface and sense rather than feel that it had grabbed my fly. At such a time one hardly has to remind oneself not to strike because by the time the line has tightened the moment has come to lift the rod anyway. It was another fine fresh fish of 13 lbs with which the steel rod coped perfectly adequately in the slowish water, but I was momentarily, and thankfully only inwardly, furious with Jock when he grabbed my line and pulled it into a tiny sidestream from which it had no escape and from which he swiftly gaffed it. I felt it was up to me to bring it to the gaff, not up to him to interfere. Later my father told me quietly that he had been worried that we were getting dangerously near the tail of the pool and had the fish opted to try to go down the run to Aultdearg, Jock felt sure that I would not have been able to hold it on my small rod and it would have been lost. Doubtless he was right.

Two days later we drove south.

Just before I returned to school my parents told me that my father was going to have an operation for the removal of a cyst from his chest. I was assured that by Long Leave he would be up and fit again and had no inkling of what was in store. During Long Leave[1] I saw him, still in hospital, already thin and sitting up with difficulty and painfully by hauling on a rope attached to the foot of his bed. Things were said to be "taking a bit longer than expected".

In another two months he was dead and the future of my fishing exploits were the last thing about which to be concerned. Nevertheless from that moment on it was certain that my salmon fishing, and probably my salmon as well, would never be more than occasional.

---

[1]Etonese for half term

25

CHAPTER THREE

ETON

Glossary:-

Half: - term
Colleger: – a scholar living in "College" rather than a normal house
Lower Boy:- a boy in his first seven to three halves at Eton
Fag:- a Lower Boy who had to do chores for older boys
M'tutor's:- my house
Library:- self electing oligarchy of "prefects" in a house (or the room they used)
Upper:- any boy not a Lower Boy
After Twelve:- a period of free time between the last morning division and Boy's Dinner
Division:- class
Beaks:- masters
M'tutor:- my house master
Field Game:- diabolically bad game of Eton football
Classical tutor:- master in charge of a boy's work
Burry:- a desk with fold down front and a cupboard on top
Early School:- first class of the day at 7.30 am
Extra Work:- prep. or any work set to be done in a boy's own time
Agar's Plough:- the main Eton cricket field
Eton Ramblers:- Old Etonian Cricket Club
Oppidans:- all boys except Collegers ie those living in normal boy's houses
XXII:- the 2nd XI (cricket only)

The best book I have ever read about everyday life at Eton is "Playing Fields: Schooldays at Eton" by Eric Parker. Although it was not written until 1922, the book is clearly autobiographical and Parker, who was a Colleger, left Eton in 1889. The extraordinary thing is that in the sixty-one years between the date he left and that at which I went to Eton in 1950 virtually nothing had changed. Of course some new buildings had appeared and after the second World War rising costs had resulted in top hats no longer being de rigueur, but, in essence, the school in my day was completely recognisable from Parker's description of it so many years before.

By contrast in the forty-seven years between 1955, when I left, and 2002 as I write this chapter, Eton itself and public schools in general have changed out of all recognition. Whether that change has been for the better is questionable.

I did not have a guaranteed place at Eton and the fact that I eventually succeeded in getting there was as a result of the efforts of my prep school, Woodcote House. Woodcote, in Windlesham, was one of the considerable number of similar schools in the area around the Berkshire/Surrey borders, amongst which were such well known places as Scaitcliffe, Ludgrove, Lambrook, Heatherdown, Eagle House and Sunningdale. We played regular matches of soccer, rugger and cricket against all these schools, generally more than holding our own: victories against Ludgrove and Sunningdale were always, however, greeted with particular pleasure.

It was, and remains today, a wonderful school where there was always a respectful and well mannered but easy and confident relationship between staff and pupils that was unusual in the fifties. This is not to say that there was not firm discipline, but while it was backed up by a system of punishments that included the cane as a last resort, it engendered respect rather than resentment. To the embarrassment of the junior matrons, general amusement was the order of the day in the communal washroom on the relatively rare occasions when a boy had a few stripes across his bottom and we accepted it as all part and parcel of life.

I loved life at Woodcote but, as was to be the case throughout my schooldays, I never found the work easy and the school was, through no fault of its own, responsible for five years of unease as far as the academic side of life at Eton was concerned. My name was not on the list of any particular housemaster and it so happened that an exact contemporary of mine at Woodcote was in exactly the same position. There was just one vacancy open and we thus found ourselves approaching Common Entrance in a head to head situation, where whichever of us did best in the exam would take that one available place and the other would miss out. Luckily I was just slightly less dim than my adversary and Woodcote's efforts resulted in my taking Upper Fourth and him being placed in Middle Fourth. Consequently I went to Eton while he had to be content with Stowe. I have never been able to look upon this with anything other than relief, but it did have the result of my entering Eton four months before my thirteenth birthday and at a higher academic level than that for which I was suited.

Entry into Eton was divide into " Removes". At the top there was "Remove" itself followed by upper, middle and lower fourth and finally, for the real blockheads, third form. The main advantage in taking a higher "Remove" on entering Eton, was that you remained a Lower Boy, and thus a fag, for a shorter time. Somebody taking Third Form was destined to fag for seven halves whereas a boy taking Upper Fourth only did so for four, and any "sap" taking "Remove" did so for only a year.

Fagging was not terribly onerous. Each boy had a fagmaster, who normally had two fags allocated to him. It was his fags' job to keep his room tidy, light his fire, produce his tea, wait on him during it and generally nanny him, but unless he was really nasty, which few of them were in M'tutor's, none of this was likely to be very unpleasant. More of a nuisance were "Boy Calls" where a member of the Library could stand outside the door of his room and shout "Bo-o-oy-y-y" as loudly as he could. At this call all the fags in the house had to run to wherever the call came from and the one who arrived last had to do whatever task was required. This was likely to be to take a note or message to someone in another house, or go down town to collect a new pair of shoes from Ganes or a pound of sausages for tea from Rowlands. Again not very onerous but it could be a nuisance if one was in the middle of something important. Incompetent fagging, which might mean anything or nothing, was a beating offence (see below) and certainly one relatively frequent reason for getting beaten up disappeared when one became an Upper.

There was another downside to obtaining a place at Eton off the General List rather than having a place earmarked for one on the list of one particular housemaster: one simply had no idea in which house one was going to end up or who one's housemaster was going to be. As he was the most important person in one's school life this could be a dire disadvantage or a huge advantage. In my case things ought to have been perfectly satisfactory but due to fate and some strange decisions on the part of the Headmaster it turned out to be a disaster. "Prick" Wickham, into whose house I went, was a good man in the truest sense of the word, who had run a solid reliable house for some years and who had an excellent reputation. Unfortunately by 1950 he was also ill. For my first two halves, though clearly very unwell, he ran the house normally, but after that he was forced to remain in the background and died shortly thereafter. For some reason which we never really fathomed, instead of a new man being appointed at once, we were faced with an interregnum period throughout most of which M'tutor's was run by Claude Taylor. Apart from the fact that he was a fine cricketer, who had made a hundred for Oxford in the Varsity match, he had little to recommend him. He was a bachelor, he was known as "oily" Claude and he commanded and received no respect from the boys. In addition he was widely, and I am sure correctly, thought to be queer. He would not use a drawing pin because he was afraid that the blunt end of the actual pin would come through the back and into his finger.

As a result of his lack of control the house lost its way and became somewhat dilatory. If this was bad then worse was to come. We eventually heard that our new permanent housemaster was to be the Rev. R.D.F.Wild. David Wild, known as "Rubberneck" simply because he had a very long neck which, rumour had it, was the result of it being stretched in Japanese prison camps, was an odd mixture. In fact he had never been in Japan and, as a chaplain, he had actually won an M.C. in Germany in the war. After being taken prisoner he had refused to remain in an officer's camp, insisting on going to a number of camps for "other ranks" in order to minister to them. It was a standing joke that escape attempts from these latter camps were redoubled as soon as it was known that he was coming! His experience and the fact that, as a man of God, he should have had, at least to some degree, a caring nature, ought to have made him an excellent housemaster. In fact he was appalling. In later life I came to have some respect for the man and by the time he died we were friends, but he had flaws in his personality which made him totally ill-suited to look after the pastoral care of 50 adolescent boys.

He was intensely moody and would sit for long periods without speaking, chewing his lip. His sense of humour was reined in to a degree where it was hard to believe that he had one, he had favourites and, worst of all, he was an extremely bad judge of character. He was married to a colourless wife who appeared to us to take virtually no interest in the house, although this was not unusual at Eton in those days, and he had three apparently rather dreary children. Doubtless they have now all made fantastic marriages and live a wonderful life of happiness and fulfilment.

He preached the most boring sermons imaginable and we always felt that if one of his boys got into some difficulty he would be the last person to be of any assistance whatsoever. When my father died during the Christmas holiday when I was 15, I heard nothing from him at all and when I returned to school in January he never mentioned the subject. For this I never forgave him.

It is odd how small incidents stick in one's mind. I remember as if it was yesterday an "After Twelve" during my last half when my great friend David Aykroyd and I had arranged to play a rackets match in the School Doubles Competition against the school 2nd pair. I was convinced that we were as good as them and that, had we boarded in a more fashionable games playing house, we would have had at any rate the odd game for the school. As a result we were desperately keen to win.

Our more experienced opponents settled better and went into a 2-0 lead but by then word had somehow spread that there was an interesting match going on and the gallery had filled up. As the underdogs we got most of the considerable support from the uncommitted. Starting to play better we took the third game but lost the fourth which brought the score to 3-1. With the spectators now roaring us on, we took control of things to level at 3-3 and I still have little doubt that, had things remained as they were, with the adrenalin flowing and the gallery firmly behind us,we would have won the final game

Unfortunately the time was now 1.25 and suddenly the gallery emptied as everyone made their way back to their houses for Boys Dinner. Immediately the atmosphere changed, the courts became quiet and the magic had gone. We lost. I always knew, but never put into words, that the fact that Wild would be sitting at the table chewing his lip in disapproval at our being late for lunch, had a most disconcerting effect on me and may well have cost us that last game. Sure enough when we finally appeared, rather sweaty, in the dining room and explained the reason for our lateness and apologised, he had neither the grace nor apparently the interest even to ask whether we had won. That just about put the tin lid on things for me as far as he was concerned, but thankfully I was in my last week or so at Eton and allowed my fury at his attitude to dissipate harmlessly. It was, of course, ludicrous, that I, who was Captain of the House at the time, should have given even a thought to being late for Boys Dinner when we were playing an important match for the honour (what an old fashioned word that sounds today) of the house. I should have taken a shower and as much time as I needed before going to the Dining Room but Wild would not have understood that either.

The fact remains, however, that M'tutor's continued to have a lot going for it. My peers were, in the main, extremely nice, if somewhat eccentric, and, almost without exception, had the good of the house constantly in mind. But we all emerged as normal human beings despite Wild's efforts rather than because of them.

There were other bad house tutors apart from David but there were also some exceptionally good ones. It cannot have been easy to get the balance right between those, like Wild, who constantly thought the worst of all his boys, and those who trawled the prep. schools for good games players in order to give their house the best chances of winning everything in sight. At a time when games played far too large a part in school life, just as the academic side does today, the result of this policy obviously put at a great disadvantage the small number of boys in that house who did not shine on the playing field. Some housemasters nevertheless managed this balancing act with aplomb and as a result were greatly respected and a place in their house much sought after.

In the fifties the assistant masters were a strange mixture. The oldest, who had, in the main, already been house tutors, were a wonderful bunch of extraordinary eccentrics upon whom we looked with gentle amusement but who were really getting well past their sell-by date.

I will mention by name just one as an example of the sort of person about whom I am talking. "Hojo" Hope-Jones taught maths. I can remember quite clearly two of his favourite problems. We were asked to say how many times "Jackie", a donkey, would have to walk round the post to which he was tethered before the rope, which was 20 yards long would all be tight round the post, which was 6 inches in diameter. It never seemed very important and certainly is not something that I have had to calculate at any point in later life. Secondly we were asked how to turn a circle into a rectangle. This question was always put to us at the end of the half and. when we had all failed to come up with the answer, "Hojo" would appear at the final division bearing a large cream filled sponge cake made by his wife. This he would proceed to cut into quarters and would re-arrange them head to tail. At once the whole thing became clear and by the time he had repeated the operation enough times to produce a piece of cake for each of the boys in the division, he did indeed have something looking very like a long narrow rectangle. We then ate the cake and went away happy and amused. There were a number of similar old characters the like of which will never be seen again.

The younger assistant masters were a mixture of excellent and bad with the former greatly in the majority. Many of them were themselves Old Etonians, a fact which some thought was bad for the school, but which we believed to be wonderful. We were, to put it mildly, turned in on Eton to an unhealthy degree and we revelled in it.

Giles St. Aubyn, who taught history, turned up at Early School[1] in a dinner jacket at least once, having just driven straight down from London after a night out. He had one of the first Jaguar XJ120's and had discovered that you could drive down the Great West Road – this was long before the M4 was even thought of - at 40, 80 or 120 mph without getting stopped by any of the myriad traffic lights. He regularly did it at 120. He once wrote in my report that he had "failed to dissuade" me from my "support of gunboat diplomacy".

E.W."Willy" Gladstone, who was my history tutor when I became a specialist, and was the grandson of the great Victorian politician, was a most charming man who, despite being a bachelor at the time, certainly ought to have had a house: however, as happened all too often with the best Eton beaks, he was whisked off to be Headmaster of some minor public school before he could be given one. He later became Chief Scout.

Brian "Bummy" Young was another Old Etonian who was clearly a man of calibre. He duly became Headmaster of Charterhouse. He was still playing the Field Game with dash and skill while I was at the school.

"Sappy" Simpson, who had been Captain of the School, was unbelievably clever. He was my classical tutor when I first went to Eton and was kindly and understanding with a dry sense of humour. He neither knew nor cared much about anything except work and I often wondered how, with this narrowness of mind, he coped with his house when he got one.

The quality of the end of half reports was a feature of Eton life and "Sappy", like Giles St. Aubyn, always wrote exceptionally good ones. He once said that I had "glowed rather than sparkled" at some aspect of a particular subject, which I regarded as an unwonted compliment.

Robert Birley, who became Headmaster shortly after the war in succession to Claude Aurelius Elliott, was known to the boys as "Red Robert" because he was strongly

---

[1] the first lesson of the day at 7.30 before breakfast

suspected of having a lot of left wing ideas. There was little doubt that these suspicions were correct, but Birley had the intelligence to move only slowly down the inevitable road that leads to reform and thus avoided upsetting too many people. The Headmastership of Eton is a government appointment and we knew that he had been selected shortly after the Attlee government had come to power and nothing that that administration did could be good in our eyes. Before I left, however, he was already beginning to bring in a number of beaks who had not been public school educated. We looked upon them, unpleasantly, with dislike. It was the case that a number measured up badly alongside the gentlemen, but some amongst them made the grade and later became accepted as part and parcel of the place.

There is no doubt that the young Etonian of the fifties was a fairly acquired, not to say unpleasant, taste. We were politically and in all our thinking somewhere to the right of Attila the Hun, appallingly racist, in favour of capital punishment for a number of crimes less than murder and thought of William Wilberforce with horror. Although most of this may have been simply for show on the surface, it was underpinned, inevitably perhaps, by a belief in the divine right of the aristocracy, to which relatively few of us actually belonged. It was amusing to see the outrage on people's faces when we propounded our views and often led to a situation where we never really knew what we actually did think.

The reverse and more attractive side of this coin was, however, that never ever was one of the "guinea pigs", who had reached Eton via an assisted place from the state school system, made to feel different, unwelcome or in any way inferior. They were accepted as being exactly the same as all the rest of us and included quite normally in everything we did.

We hoped against hope that the awful Attlee government would fail to be re-elected in 1950 and though disappointed when it struggled back to power with a tiny majority, we knew enough about the workings of the Commons to realise that this would shortly be put right. In due course it was and Churchill returned to 10 Downing

Street in 1951. Despite the fact that he was an Old Harrovian, he was everybody's hero.

*   *   *

One of the main things that made Eton so different from other public schools was the fact that every boy in the school had a room of his own from his first day there. To start with it was generally a small one, perhaps about 10 ft x 8 ft into which were snugly fitted a burry, a small table, an upright chair and also a comfortable reclining arm chair. There was also a washstand and, naturally, a bed which, during the day swung up sideways or endwise out of the way. Most memorable to Old Etonians there was also the inevitable Eton ottoman which contained one's games clothes. From this a smell of appalling stale sweat emerged whenever it was opened. On the wall was a sock[1] cupboard containing everything one needed for tea.

In most of the more ancient and much more characterful buildings, the older boys got bigger and better rooms as they progressed through the school and many ended up with something measuring 15 ft square or more. These were genuine bed-sitting rooms of considerable comfort.

I started my time at the College in a modern house called "Mustians", built in 1937. Not only was it on the fringe of the town, being virtually the last house down Dorney Road, but also it was prison-like in its austerity. Every room was about the same size and it had three almost identical landings. At one end of each of these was a staircase surrounded by prison railings. When Wild took over we were moved to what was thought to be the worst house in the school – Carter House. This was central, being situated just opposite College Chapel, rambling in the extreme and had barely two rooms on the same level. One or two steps up and down were everywhere, it was full of character and very few rooms were the same as any other. Before I was sixteen I had a charming room measuring about 12 ft. square that many people of my

---

[1] tuck in most schools' languages

age would have been pleased to have had at home and the whole building had a cosy feel of friendliness. Sadly it has now been condemned and is no longer a boy's house. They have to make do with another modern monstrosity devoid of personality or feeling. Progress!

Each boy could decorate his room in whatever way he wished, with pictures and curtains to his own taste, but the fad for large posters, particularly the one of the back view of the girl tennis player, which became such a favourite years later, had not yet arrived. It would certainly would not have found much favour with such humourless housemasters as David Wild.

Most importantly there was an open fireplace. We were allocated one bundle of kindling wood and two small buckets of coal each week. Each bucket would allow one to have three small and, as most people thought, inadequate and pointless fires, two good ones or one massive one. Most people went for the middle option and spent the evenings in a friend's room when they did not have a fire of their own. Learning how to light a good fire naturally became a vital part of life and few people are as good at it in after life as are older Old Etonians.

On the inevitable occasions when things went wrong and the fire did not "draw" properly, the thing to do was to "bumph it up". This consisted of getting hold of a whole newspaper, preferably the Times which did not catch fire so easily as cheaper publications, and cover the whole aperture of the fireplace with it, leaving a small gap of an inch or so at the bottom. This created a fierce draught which always resulted in the fire flaring up immediately. Unfortunately it would generally die down again just as quickly when the paper was removed, so that the trick was to keep it in place until you had a veritable inferno roaring up the chimney. For some reason the chimney itself never seemed to catch fire.

One waited like this for as long as one dared without the paper catching fire. If it did so the only possible course was to fold the flaming newsheet into as small a ball as one could without getting burnt and shove the whole thing into the fireplace. How we never managed to set the whole house on fire I cannot imagine, but there was never even the smallest dangerous incident that I can recall.

On nights when one had no fire one just had a cold room. There was no other form of heating and, as it was inevitably the case that most boys, during their early days, went through the odd short period when they were not flavour of the month with their contemporaries and were thus unwelcome in anyone else's room. this did lead to a somewhat miserable time. Such periods were, however, normally very short lived.

Everyday life at Eton began at 6.45 am when there was a knock on the door of one's room and without, waiting for an answer, the Boys' Maid entered with a jug of hot water for washing and shaving, which she dumped on the washstand with a dreadfully cheerful "Mornin' Mr. Reynolds. Quarter to seven, dear. Very cold". About 7.15 one tumbled out of bed, shaved and dressed and somehow got to Early School by 7.30. Division rooms were spread all over the town so that a house in the centre near College Chapel was a distinct advantage.

At 8.15 we returned to our tutor's for breakfast which, after an interval which just gave us enough time to visit the "rears"[1] was followed by a short compulsory chapel service. Two further divisions followed and at 11.45 boys in the Upper School were free until Boys Dinner at 1.30. Lower Boys had to attend "pupil room" where their classical tutor, who was theoretically in charge of the academic side of their life, oversaw them doing any work set to be completed in out of school hours. "After Twelves" were a favourite time for individual non-team games like fives, rackets and squash to be played, but one could fill the time in any way one wished. Organised team games took place on Tuesday, Thursday and Saturday afternoons when there was no work, but on Monday, Wednesday or Friday afternoons there were two further "divs". These took place either immediately after lunch or, in the winter, just before dark when "lock-up" meant that all boys had to be back in their houses. After that they

---

[1] loo

could only emerge with a "House Ticket" authorising them to go to some Society meeting or event.

In winter tea took place just after lock-up and two or three boys messed together in the room of one of them, providing between them all sorts of goodies from eggs to Baxter's Royal Game Soup – which always had, and still has today, some shot in it to prove that it was made from real birds! -and from lemon curd to Tiptrees strawberry jam . The first course was cooked, with a great deal of hassle, on a few gas rings in each passage.

The evenings were again free time although a good deal of extra work had to be fitted in and the Lower Boys were regimented to the extent of there being a "Quiet Hour" during which they had to be in their own room, unless they had permission to share another's, and were expected to work rather than chat.

Sundays were different. There was compulsory chapel both in the morning and evening and unless a boy had permission to be away for the day, Boys' Dinner had to be attended. There were no games and the rest of the day was free. People sat around and discussed, or more often argued about, the important matters of the day. This was a very favourite Etonian pastime. Sometimes one walked up to Windsor or to the Castle. One was said not to be a proper Etonian until one had walked to the "Copper Cow": this was an equestrian statue about three miles up the Long Walk beyond Windsor Castle and past the Frogmore Mausoleum. There never seemed to be time to do this on any other day of the week.

*   *   *

The two great special days in the Eton calendar were 4th June celebrating the birth of George III, in whose memory Etonians still wear tail coats and stripey trousers as a sign of mourning, and St. Andrews Day on 30th November.

Provided the weather was kind 4th June was a lovely day. Parents and siblings arrived in time for mid morning Absence and then repaired to Agar's Plough, where the XI would be playing the Eton Ramblers. Guests and boys alike perambulated round the ground, talking to friends and relations, everyone in their smartest clothes, the ladies wearing hats, younger sisters in frilly dresses and older ones demure and delightful. The cricket was incidental. A picnic lunch in the long grass at the side of the ground followed, generally accompanied by yelps of dismay from females of all ages who found their stockings irrevocably marked with oil off the undersides of the cars that littered the surrounding area.

The Brigade of Guards', or perhaps the Greenjackets', Band played the popular songs of the moment and doe eyed debs looked longingly into the faces of their O.E. debs' delight escorts. Current Etonians dillied and dallied with girl friends if they were lucky enough to have one who had been let out of her own boarding school for the day. Soon it would be time for a quick visit to the exhibition in the Drawing Schools or something similar before each boy took his parents and guests back to tea in his room.

In the early evening the first Procession of Boats took place off Fellows Eyot. At Evening Absence all the serious rowers in the school who had been awarded rowing colours of some sort, paraded in their old style naval uniforms, the diminutive coxes dressed as Admirals with fore-and-aft hats and carrying bouquets of flowers. Once on the river they yelled commands at their crew as they rowed, first upstream until out of sight of the watching crowds, then turned and, getting up speed, stopped rowing, and in pairs raised their oars vertically and stood up. Finally they were left with no oars in the water to balance the boat. This was an athletic feat of some proportions. Surprisingly few boats ever turned over though the spectators willed them to do so.

After dinner, as dusk fell, the highlight of the day took place. Virtually everyone traipsed back to Fellows Eyot, jockeying good naturedly for a good position, and sat on a rug on the grass, perhaps finishing a picnic supper and almost always drinking more than was good for them.

Finally, darkness having descended and impatience starting to grow, the first of the boats again shot upstream, picked out by the floodlights. Each boat's crew wore a different colour and it was a memorable scene. After the return trip downstream, which provided another chance to see a disaster as the crews repeated their balancing act, and with the Band playing The Eton Boating Song, all went dark and the fireworks started. The display was accepted as one of the best anywhere and it was always a wonderful finale to the day. Towards the end there would be a series of huge rockets, the first of which burst with a single starshell, the second with two and so on up to nine or ten, while the crowd roared out the numbers. "O-o-n-n-e." "O-o-n-n-e, t-t-w-w-o-o" until we were all hoarse. Firework pictures of the King and Queen and then, later in my time there, the Queen and Prince Philip followed while the Band played and we sang the National Anthem.

As the Eton coat of arms appeared through the smoke we wandered back towards our houses, said goodbye to our parents and family, feeling that we were indeed at "the best of schools". "Smug" is probably the adjective that summed us up best.

*   *   *

By contrast with 4th June St. Andrews Day on 30th November was a fairly awful occasion. It was always wet, muddy and foggy. The dreadful, pointless and incomprehensible Wall Game was played between the Collegers and Oppidans and one longed for the day to end. Visitors never enjoyed it much and the fact that I cannot remember much about it must mean that it had little to recommend it.

It was the only occasion on which members of "Pop" wandered around in public with their badge of office, their canes, in their hands. Surprisingly nobody took any notice.

Far better than St. Andrew's Day in the 1950's was Lord's. In those days the Eton and Harrow match was a high spot of the London season. The ground was packed over the full two days of the game and, apart from the boys who wore ordinary suits, all the men were in morning dress and the ladies wore their most dramatic summer dresses with hats a l'Ascot. The cricket, unlike that on 4th June, was fiercely partisan and groups of Etonians and Harrovians gathered in certain parts of the ground, giving loud but friendly support to their team and trying to outdo the noise from the opposition.

So packed was the ground that to walk round it was a feat of endurance. The limited space under the old grandstand might take 20 minutes to get through and the Nursery End was covered with picnic parties, the arbours all full of longstanding tenants for the fixture. Round the boundary, coaches (old fashioned horse drawn affairs) were parked, giving a wonderful view to those sitting atop them and effectively blocking any sight of the wicket to those behind them. In the intervals between play, the gates in the boundary fences were opened and everyone paraded round the outfield.

Stories of battles between the two sets of boys in the past were still on the lips of the older men but by now such behaviour had long since passed into memory and it was an occasion of total decorum.

How sadly changed things are today. Gone are the 4th June fireworks, deemed too expensive. Gone is the floodlit Procession of Boats, deemed too dangerous after some fools, either O.E.'s or a party of yobs from Slough, depending on which story you want to believe, swam out to the boats one year and tried to tip them all over.

Lord's too! No morning dress, no crowds, little interest, the two day game truncated to a limited overs match played in a day.

St. Andrews Day may be much the same but I doubt whether many people bother to go to it to find out.

*   *   *

I suppose that the discipline was very similar in the fifties to that still in force today. Everything was pretty easy going but there were marks that one overstepped at one's peril and one knew perfectly well where those marks were. The system was divided between school discipline, duly subdivided into that enforced by the beaks on the one hand and the boys on the other, and house discipline.

School discipline covered, as far as the beaks were concerned, work, or lack of it, and the obvious things like smoking, drinking, gambling, being out of bounds or the constantly talked about but rarely if ever, at least in M'tutor's, carried out, acts of indecency. (Most older boys had crushes on a younger one, but in general this was all amusing talk and action was neither contemplated nor desired.) Pop, the self electing body of school prefects, only became involved if people misbehaved in the street or town which was incredibly rare. More often messing around took place on the river where questions of safety had to be considered and where the Captain of Boats, who was an ex-officio member of Pop, ruled supreme.

House discipline was enforced by another self elected oligarchy known as the "Library" which consisted of five or six of the senior boys in each house.

"Poenas" fifty years ago were very different from the appallingly liver livered and often ineffectual "sanctions" imposed today. Although very far from barbaric the whole system was underpinned by corporal punishment of various sorts. The Headmaster used a range of punishments before resorting to flogging. He could order a boy to do a Georgic which consisted of copying out about 500 lines of Latin verse, or could issue a yellow, or worse, a white, ticket which meant that a boy's behaviour and work was closely watched during the period of the ticket, normally about 14 days. If he did anything wrong during that time a flogging generally resulted. I am told that this was minimally painful but, as it was administered with a birch, it was always given on the bare buttocks and thus involved a degree of humiliation.

Pop could fine a boy up to five shillings – a considerable sum – or in extreme circumstances summon the culprit for a "pop tanning". This was serious. Pop canes were vicious implements, knobbly and very flexible and the victim was made to bend over with his head on a window sill, the sash window then being lowered on the back of his neck. He was always told to attend in an old pair of trousers as the cane would do them, as well as his backside, a good deal of damage. Pop tanning was very, very rare.

In their houses boys could be fined by the Library, probably threepence or sixpence for small misdemeanours. More serious breaches of discipline were punished by a "beating up". The wrongdoer would be summoned to the library (the room in which the afore mentioned oligarchy passed their time) after prayers, given a lecture about his iniquities and then told to wait outside the door. The noise of furniture being moved around could be heard while one waited and at a shout of "come" one went in and bent over the back of a chair to receive four, six or occasionally more strokes from a house cane. These were lightweight implements that could be bought at Thomas's the hairdressers in the High Street where they lay openly in a glass topped counter. Being beaten up was not a disaster. It was briefly painful but soon over and forgotten.

I can remember two completely different school crimes committed by boys in M'tutor's. The first was laughable and showed Wild up in a very poor light. A great friend of mine, Mick Whitaker. went to m'dame and obtained an order for a new razor. Orders were available to purchase small items, the cost of which would then be added to the boy's school bill. Going to the chemist, Mick produced the order but instead of buying a normal safety razor he took away an electric one made by a firm called KUB. This was, of course, far more expensive. Mick maintained that his action was entirely reasonable – it was a razor and the order was for a razor so where was the problem? M'tutor chose to think that he was being dishonest and promoted a major row. As Mick was an extraordinary character anyway (he used to thrust out his hand whenever anyone disagreed with him saying in a high pitched squeal "Bet you £5" – he once did it when we told him he could not jump safely out of a first floor window using an umbrella as a parachute and had to be dissuaded from trying) it all seemed rather unimportant. It became known as the "KUB Row" and was laughingly referred to as such for years to come.

More serious was an incident where two boys in the house, who fancied themselves as antique experts, which one of them later became, walked down the High Street and surreptitiously removed a large china bull from an antique shop. They then crossed the road and sold it to a similar shop a few doors higher up. It was only when the owner of the first shop saw his bull in the opposition's window that he noticed it had disappeared. The two boys in question also disappeared next day. Our feelings were that they deserved all they got, particularly in view of their incredible stupidity.

It was with Mick Whitaker that I became one of the last Etonians to swim in the Thames. Even as high up the river as Windsor it was pretty filthy and rumour had it that bathing at Cuckoo Weir was shortly to be stopped. This was during the summer when polio was rife throughout the country and the school eventually succumbed when one boy died and a number of others contracted more or less serious strains of the potentially fatal disease. There was a good deal of talk about it being caused by dirty water and eventually, as I remember, this was proved to be the case. Before that happened, however, Mick and I took ourselves off one warm afternoon and, where generations of Etonians before us had done the same, we swam.

I cannot pretend it was much fun. Today the river supports salmon again, and the past fifty years have seen a massive clean up but in 1953 it was absolutely filthy. It was all too easy to imagine that the various bits of detritus floating past ones eyes at close range were indeed human sewage and we had no wish to repeat the performance that within a couple of weeks was forbidden. Nowadays the College boasts two swimming pools but then it had none. It was a strange anomaly that a school that offered so much still provided nowhere for the boys to swim in safety.

There are so many good Eton stories that it is hard to know which are apocryphal and which are genuinely true. I suspect that most start with a strong element of truth in them and become enhanced, embellished and exaggerated as they are passed from mouth to mouth. Some, the best of them, do not need that treatment.

Towards the end of my last summer half M'tutors were drawn against the hot favourites for the cricket House Sides. Mr. Wykes's team boasted no fewer than five members of that years Eton XI plus the 12th man. Against this array of talent we could only put into the field one member of the XXII and one much younger player who would eventually become 12th man to the XI a year later. The rest of our side was made up of no hopers.

It was clear that as a contest it was not a starter and as you can imagine we won the game easily. For some reason an extraordinary fellow named Hughie Crofton, who was quite batty but was a good friend of mine, umpired for most of the game. Our one good player bowled fastish off breaks and amongst his other wickets were a number of lbw's, the decisions on which were given by Hughie. I have no reason to believe that they were anything other than perfectly honest and good decisions and the opposition gave no sign at the time that they were particularly upset by them.

Once the match was over, however, Hughie received a note from Wykes himself reading:-

Dear Crofton,
Before you umpire another game of cricket it would be best if you acquainted yourself with the lbw law.
Sincerely, N.G.Wykes.

Nigel Wykes was one of the worst amongst those housemasters who trawled the prep schools for accomplished games players and the enjoyment of the whole school at the discomfiture of his house over this game of cricket was too much for him. Hughie, however, was quite equal to the challenge. He immediately wrote a reply and sent it round to Mr. Wykes by a fag. His note read:-

Dear Wykes,(sic)
I have received your note. I enclose herewith my certificate of accreditation as an umpire approved by the Hampshire County Cricket Club. Please make certain that it is returned to me before lock-up tonight.
Yours, Crofton.

The matter was not raised again.

Oddly enough another story concerned the same two houses drawn against each other once again the following summer. By then Wykes's apparent superiority had diminished somewhat but this time they made no mistake. By tea on the last day of the game three innings had been completed and they needed just 12 runs to win in the final innings. The game, like most senior house matches, was being played on one of the pitches on the outfield of Agar's Plough, the main Eton ground, which is about 15 minutes walk from the school. M'tutor's being unwilling to concede the game, it was therefore necessary for the players to return to their houses for tea and then traipse up to Agar's again to finish the game. Wykes's decided that it would be enough to send up four players, their opening pair plus two others to umpire and to replace the opening batsmen in the unlikely event of them losing a wicket . It is not hard to guess what happened. They quickly lost three wickets, had no further batsmen available to come in and lost by default. Mr. Wykes cannot have been overjoyed.

As I have said M'tutor was not a popular figure in the school. In addition to his other shortcomings his sermons were unbelievably dreadful. One day a year or two after I left, it was decided – by whom I know not – to play a most unkind joke on him. It was the custom at early communion for all those boys who wished to take the sacrament to place their penny, or sixpence or trouser button, in the collection bag and then kneel down. If one did not kneel it was a sign that one did not wish to take communion. On this particular day there were, astonishingly, not the usual fifty or so boys in College Chapel but about three hundred, all of who duly knelt after the collection. David Wild was taking the service and was put aback when the "Holy Poker"[1] whispered to him that there were 315 prospective communicants. He duly blessed enough bread and wine to cater for this unusually high number only to find that just 15 people, mainly beaks and their wives, appeared at the altar rail.

---

[1] verger

He was now faced with enough communion wine, duly blessed, for 300 people which, even at a tiny sip each, amounted to a considerable quantity. Nobody could have accused him of not being brave. He downed the lot, did the washing up and fell down the steps leading from the altar to the choir.

When I first heard this story I sincerely doubted its authenticity. This year, however, a source completely new to me confirmed that it was true.

Perhaps the best thing about being an Old Etonian is that one can come across fellow O.E's in the most unlikely places and at the most unlikely times – it is in fact just a rather good club.

With that in mind the best Eton story I have heard for years was told to me by a good friend at a dinner party recently. When he was about 15 he was given, totally unjustly as he thought, a hell of a beating by the Captain of his house, an individual with a most distinctive surname preceded by three distinctive initials. Thirty years later when my friend was Chairman of the Bench somewhere in London, the name of one defendant, who was accused of failing to stop after a road accident and who had the same distinctive name and initials, jumped out of the list of cases at him. When the case in question came on, he knew he would have to withdraw: he leant over to tell his fellows on the Bench that, though he had known this chap and clearly could not sit in judgement on him, he was no friend of his. Before he could get this message across his erstwhile tormenter's solicitor got to his feet and asked him to leave the bench while the case was heard. Deprived of the opportunity to communicate with his co-magistrates he nevertheless returned after the case was finished, confident that the bearer of this distinctive name would have finally received his come uppance. To his dismay his colleague whispered to him "We managed to find a way of letting your friend off"!

*   *   *

The main planks of an Eton education remain in place today, but a lot of the best things from the 1950's have been swept away in the drive to modernise the public schools. Nevertheless this has lead to a watering down of many of the best things about them. Sadly a lot of what has gone from Eton, while perhaps small in themselves, are things that made the College just that little bit different and (dare I say it?) a little bit better than other schools.

Of course, in common with all schools, fagging and all forms of corporal punishment have passed into history but other changes, seemingly unimportant to non-Etonians, are more depressing.

The floodlit procession of boats and the wonderful fireworks of 4th June will never be seen again. "Lord's" is a pale shadow of the wonderful match it used to be. Worst of all the summer half has become little more than drudgery, a tramp towards the inevitable "A" levels that leaves little time for more important things like cricket and rowing or for chatting and growing up, discussing and broadening one's mind, and becoming, in fact, a person. Coal fires have gone to be replaced by central heating and all the new houses have been built with standard sized rooms, removing the individualistic character of the older buildings. For most houses Boy's Dinner is now served in a central dining hall, where boys from all the houses have lunch communally in some awful sort of buffet. Presumably table manners, never wonderful, have suffered further as a result.

But the cache of having had an Eton education, for better or worse, remains. I have heard it said that it is today actually a disadvantage. This I beg leave to doubt.

CHAPTER FOUR

IRISH INTERLUDE

After leaving school and spending a year abroad, with the idea of learning French and Spanish, which met with total lack of success, and during which time I was appallingly unhappy and spent the whole time longing to be back in England, I went to work in the City in 1957 at the age of 19.

Fishing had taken a back seat since my father's death, although my mother had done her best to alleviate my feeling of desolation by taking me back to the Carnarvon Arms in the holidays. There were too many memories there for us to be happy and once we tried the White Hart in Launceston, Cornwall, where we fished the Tamar, which was constantly in spate throughout the week. We did not repeat the exercise.

I could not put into words and she either did not understand or, more likely, understood all too well, that fishing was unfulfilling for me without my father around.

I had some friends who shot which I did not. I knew a few people, both boys and girls, who hunted and met a lot more during the London Seasons of 1957 and 1958 in which I got fairly involved, but I never came across anyone who fished. This led to a vacuum that it was hard to fill and, as the social side of London life became less hectic and less fulfilling, I began to look around for places to go off to fish by myself. The easiest way to do this was to find hotel water where I could fish at a realistic cost and not be too lonely while doing so. Fishing is in essence a solitary sport and being by nature something of a loner, this aspect did not worry me too much.

Accordingly I scoured the Field and similar publications for hotels advertising fishing and went for a week to Bracken Bank at Lazonby on the Eden. As I found neither the hotel nor the other guests particularly friendly and there was no water in the river anyway, this was not a success but, through a Yorkshire school friend, I had met a lovely girl who lived at Mallow in Co. Cork after whom I lusted at a safe distance. She was for a short time in the Irish Three Day Event team of which her father was the senior member, once nearly slitting his throat when he took the wrong course in the Show jumping phase, thus getting the whole team disqualified when they were assured of at least a bronze medal at the Olympics. The family offered me a couple of days fishing on their stretch of the Blackwater and I was thus enticed to find some other salmon fishing in the south of Ireland for a week to make up ten days holiday during the summer of 1960. The Irish Tourist Board produced a pile of brochures from hotels offering salmon fishing from which I chose, with complete lack of knowledge as to what I was looking for, The Glencar Hotel in Co. Kerry. It was to prove a choice as varied as the proverbial curate's egg.

I arrived at the hotel on a hot, dry August day and for a week the sky remained a brilliant blue and the river sank ever lower. I quickly discovered that everyone fishing the Upper Caragh River spun. A fly was regarded as useless and although I put up a fly rod and wandered up and down the length of the river, manfully maintaining that if there had been water in the river fish would take a fly as well as anything else, it was not hard to see why I was in a minority of one amongst the six or seven other frustrated fishing guests. Although most of the pools had a decent run into the head of them, practically all of them quickly became too deep, for a fly to reach down to the fish. The flow then ran out into deep dead water on both sides of the pool almost immediately instead of fanning out over the full width of the river or running down one bank. There was little room for optimism for anyone that week nor, for me as a fly fisherman, for the future, but I was immensely and relaxedly happy there.

I spent a lot of time walking to various lakes where I could cast a fly contentedly for hours, sometimes even catching a reasonable number of 6-8 oz trout. I remember particularly the Red Lakes where the bottom actually did appear red through almost blood coloured water and the trout had a scarlet hue to them. Another lake named Drumbrain was reported to hold huge trout but was surrounded by reeds to such an extent that one could not get a fly satisfactorily into it. A year or so later, when most people at the hotel knew me relatively well and at a time when fish were proving impossible to catch, I told Nora Daly, the proprietress, that I was thinking of going over to Drumbrain. By the time I returned to the hotel in the evening I was amazed to be met with undue enthusiasm by the owner to whom my comment had been translated as "Mr. Reynolds is thinking of drowning himself". The Irish accent in Kerry was very broad.

The pub itself was a charming place with views in one direction to Macgillycuddy's Reeks in the distance ands in the other to Carrauntoohil, Ireland's highest mountain. Killorglin, the nearest small town was out of another era with few cars and lots of donkey carts pulled by animals in a variety of states of health but including some whose feet had clearly had no attention for literally years, which upset me a great deal. Jack and Nora Daly, the hotel owners, were charming people. Of course it took time to get to know them but, by the end of my first fishless week there, it was clear to me that Glencar was a place where I could happily stay again. The restrictive nature of the fishing, where each beat consisted of two or in some cases even one pool, and the fact that spinning was clearly the only likely method that might yield a fish, took second place in my mind to the advantage of finding somewhere where I could enjoy myself on my own without feeling awkward or lonely in any way. As a result I determined to return in the spring when I was informed that the main run of salmon took place and one could be almost assured of getting adequate water.

I returned to London deeply depressed to be back and it was from that moment that I knew I should not be working there and started to seriously hanker after a job in the country. It took me a further 19 years to achieve this modest goal.

In April 1961 I returned to Glencar. I took the ferry from Fishguard to Rosslare on an appallingly stormy night. I had an inside cabin and the boat rolled and pitched alarmingly throughout the crossing. I had almost got used to the irregular motion, which, for some reason, did not make me feel at all sick, when there was an enormous bang as if we had hit something solid. I had visions of this ferry ending up at the bottom of the Irish Sea like the Princess Victoria a few years before and was convinced that I would not be able to escape from my cabin, which certainly felt as if it was well below the waterline. It seemed best therefore to stay in my bunk and just wait to drown. Of course the boat just resumed its earlier motion having presumably hit nothing more solid than an extra large wave and we duly docked at Rosslare on time. I had no option but to return by the same route on which I and my car were booked but never again went to Ireland by sea.

The storm which had, as I thought, nearly sunk the ferry, had brought plenty of rain to Southern Ireland and I drove down to Kerry through floods and across rivers swollen to their banks. Many of these streams were simply full of mud brown spate water in which fishing would clearly be impossible for days to come and I rued the fact that while last summer there had been no water, the spring had brought me back to Ireland when there was surely to be far too much. Remembering how quickly the Glenarm and the Tilt had cleared after a spate, and indeed how clear their waters had remained even after the heaviest rain, I tried to remain hopeful that the Upper Caragh would show the same characteristics. Flowing as it did out of Lake Cloon only a few miles upstream from the hotel, there seemed a good chance that it would retain a degree of clarity however full it became. Unlike those lowland rivers that meandered through farmland picking up every sort of dirt and muddiness on their way, rivers that rise in mountainous country generally remain clear, if deep whisky (or should it be whiskey as this is about Ireland?) coloured, however high they are running.

On getting to Glencar that was what I found to be the case. The guests were rubbing their hands in expectation of a bonanza as soon as the river dropped just a little and I was assured that fish would be there for the taking tomorrow, or possibly the day after!

It is only now thinking back on it that I realise how incredibly restricted the fishing was at Glencar. From the hotel a steep track, about half a mile long, led down to the river where it emerged from the woods at the side of the Boat Pool. Upstream from here there were a few nice pools but in the main they yielded few fish with the exception of a dreary flat stretch known as the Leens. There was little or no flow there at whatever height the river happened to be, but fish did lie in the slack water and took rather well under the sully bushes on both sides of the river.

The Boat Pool itself – despite its name there was no boat - was deemed the best one on the river and was about 100 yards long with a nice stream at the top, which broadened, in good water, into a wide, flat, deep, rather slow pool before quickening again near the lip. The top and best part of the pool could be easily reached with a fly from the bank but was never fished with anything other than a spinner. Below this the river was unfishable until it emerged from a series of shallow runs into another flat canal-like pool. This was known as Long Range. At the bottom a small tributary ran into the main river and the pool thus formed was called Joinings. Further down was a large round pool, Flag Pool, where the water swirled uncontrollably making a fly virtually impossible to fish and this gave way to Kennedys which was more easily managed but rather featureless. Finally the bottom pool on the river was Blackstones which was fishable with a fly and contained some rather nice water at the top and a good lip at the draw .

When I say that the whole of this stretch of river was divided into seven beats, four of which ran from the top of the Boat Pool to the bottom of Blackstones you will see that each beat was incredibly short. Despite starting with enthusiasm to fish my beat each day with a fly, and actually momentarily hooking a fish in Blackstones on one, it soon became clear to me that, if I was going to give myself a realistic chance of catching a fish or two, I was going to have to spin. I and my fellow fishers thus spent most of each day hurling a minnow into a patch of water not greatly larger than a council house lawn. Looking back on it now it seems unbelievable that for five years running I did this rather than find somewhere else to go. But I did and the reason was simple: I liked my fellow guests and the proprietors and the general atmosphere of the place so much that having "got into it" I did not want to start finding my feet somewhere else.

This feeling of well being was undoubtedly heightened by the fact that I actually did catch a fish. My beat for the day was Long Range and Joinings which was really one long narrow still sort of pool, the top of which was featureless while in the tail, where the tributary stream entered the main river thus providing a little extra flow, there were a number of huge submerged rocks which clearly provided good lies. It was at this point that I hooked the fish on a brown and gold minnow. I had no idea what to do with it as it was the first time that I had ever felt a salmon on a spinning rod. Setting the slipping clutch on a fixed spool reel had to be done by trial and error. To begin with I found that I had set it too loose and however hard I reeled in nothing happened. As soon as I realised this I tightened it up to a point where the fish could not take any line at all. With 20 lb breaking strain nylon and the usual large treble hooks associated with bait fishing, there seemed no great disadvantage in this, a mistake that was to cost me dear a year or so later. However my fly fishing training soon led to my loosening the clutch again to a position that seemed close to providing the same sort of check that one would get on a fly reel. From then on I played the fish in exactly the same way as I would have done on a fly rod.

Having overcome this initial problem it was time to start worrying about how to land it. The four salmon I had caught while my father was alive had all been gaffed for me and I was far from certain how I was going to manage to unhook the gaff from my belt, extend it, get the fish into a position in which it was presenting its side to me and within my reach and get it ashore without dropping the rod. I managed it eventually as it was happily well hooked and was unpleasantly self satisfied at having achieved my first self gaffed fish. It was a fresh 11 lb springer and was my first salmon for nine years.

Despite having no more fish that year my intention of returning to Glencar was reinforced when I fell in with a very charming chap named Maj. Brassey-Gottlieb. He seemed old to me then but was probably not more than about fifty five! He had spent his working years in East Africa, presumably born of German antecedents left behind when Tanganyika was ceded to Britain at the end of the first world war. We shared a table in the dining-room and drank together a good deal. He had a good range of stories from his colonial days including several based on fishing for Nile perch which apparently had to be winched from great depths by sheer strength. As they could weigh up to 300 lbs this required a bit of serious effort.

Every night after dinner we used to buy each other a liqueur, starting on the bottle at one end of the bar and progressing, as the week went by, towards the other. It is the only time I have downed a glass of green Chartreuse and quickly chased it with one of yellow! The green is far better – and a good deal more expensive. Even in those days it cost 2/6d.[1]

Before leaving we both made a booking to return the following spring in the same week and any chance there might have been of my finding some better fishing had disappeared.

*   *   *

When I went back to Glencar in 1962 the Dalys had obtained some water on the River Laune a few miles away at Killorglin which provided a welcome change from the restricted beats on the Upper Caragh. Joe had heard that the fish were running and that there was plenty of water and I was despatched to fish the single beat to which the hotel had access. In retrospect I realise that at a lower level this water would have been perfect for a fly but at spring height and in view of the necessity, as I was informed, of getting the bait well down in the water, there seemed no alternative but to spin again. There were two main pools and from the top one, Col-ha-noor, I took two fish on the first day and followed them with a third on the following day. They were all fresh run, two were covered in sea lice and, as they weighed in at 8, 15, and 11 lbs respectively, they took some landing on my

_____

[1] 12 ½ p

own in the heavy water. By now, however, I seemed to have got the hang of the wretched clutch and was confident enough of my gaff work not to worry overmuch about getting them on the bank.

After that I was consigned back to the Caragh, deemed to have had my share of the Laune beat and strange to say nobody else had a fish off it for the rest of that week. A number were taken off the "home" river but not by me. The most successful angler was a brash young Englishman called Bowling. He was noisy, boring and full of himself and was naturally nicknamed "Tombolling" by the rest of the guests. As he clearly knew nothing at all about fishing, it was irritating to find him regularly bringing salmon home, but it was only towards the end of the week that we discovered that he was habitually fishing with his minnow spinning the wrong way up!

There were a couple of gillies attached to the hotel and he could clearly have done with the assistance of one of them – although, come to think of it, he did perfectly well on his own. One of these gillies was a dour, dreary man named, appropriately, Macgillycuddy, whom I remember mainly for an unfortunate episode that I had one day when I took a boat out on Cloon Lake at the top of the Caragh system with him as my boatman. The approved and dreadful method of fishing the lake from a boat was for the fisherman to be rowed round and round it with two baits trailing out of the back, waiting for a fish to take. It was dull in the extreme and made the more so by Macgillycuddy's unwaveringly stern countenace, which only broke into something near approachability when he was offered my whiskey flask. In the middle of he afternoon we finally hooked a fish. I played it dead and brought it alongside the boat at which point Mac discovered that he had left his net behind. I handed him my gaff, he stuck it into the fish which promptly slipped off it and a moment later the hooks came away. Deep silence prevailed and another blank day went into the records.

The other gillie, whose name I cannot recall, was a very different character but no less of a liability. If his guest hooked a fish he used to run excitedly up and down the bank shouting alternatively "Let her run, let her run!" followed by "Pull her head off, pull her head off!". As the fisherman never took any notice of either instruction no great harm was ever done but it was not relaxing. This man used to drink huge quantities of Guinness in the hotel bar each night. If he stopped before reaching his twentieth pint he could normally cycle home, but if he went over this limit he never got beyond the end of the drive. Here he hurled his bicycle into the bushes and curled up for the night. Without returning home, he would then be seen next morning pushing his bike back up to the hotel to begin another days work as if nothing abnormal had happened.

1963's trip to Glencar was a most unsatisfactory one. The first day I was there I asked if I could go back to the Laune and arrived there to find the river seemingly in perfect condition. This appeared to be confirmed by the fact that, within the first few casts, I hooked another fresh run fish of around 10 lbs. Over confidence is a bad fault when playing a salmon, particularly on a spinning rod, the stiffness of which tends to remove the guidance that the flexibility of a fly rod gives you about the strength of the fish and its readiness for landing. In addition, by screwing down the slipping clutch beyond a certain level, one gives the fish no leeway at all and can easily find oneself reeling in a still strong salmon without realising that one is putting on far more pressure than is justified or intended. Doubtless those who habitually use these fixed spool reels find themselves able to adjust to this danger without too much difficulty. Suffice to say that on this occasion I hauled the poor fish to the bank far too quickly and, finding it slipping downstream in the strong water as I reached down for it with the gaff, simply tightened the clutch up until it was solid. The result was inevitable. The line broke at the swivel two foot above the minnow.

I suppose that this would have been disaster enough whatever was to come afterwards, but when the rest of that day proved blank and was followed by six more blank days on the Upper Caragh, I spent a long time ruing my mistake and returning to England fishless was not a happy experience. Although I went back to Glencar for three further years it was

57

to prove the last fish I hooked on either river over there. I did land four more salmon in Co. Kerry but they were all taken from Cloon Lake at the top of the Caragh system and as two of them were kelts it was not a good period in my salmon fishing life. The first kelt was a long thin bar of silver. I suppose that I knew it was not a fresh fish but as, in the way that kelts often do, it had taken the minnow with such gusto that it ended up halfway down its throat, there was no way I could either get it out nor release the fish with it still there. I thus knocked it on the head, took it quietly back to the hotel and let Joe Daly confirm it as a kelt and quietly bury it. He duly cut out my minnow and returned it to me.

Only a couple of days later I caught another one that was just as thin as the first but not so clean. This time I was able to release it easily enough and with the very next cast hooked a clean fish that I was able to kill with a clear conscience. As is sometimes the case it seemed certain that the two fish had been lying near each other and the fact that the kelt moved violently when it was hooked duly woke up the other one.

Although Cloon was a most beautiful place to pass a day, being surrounded on three sides by high hills with only the outlet end falling away over low lying ground, and despite having another fresh, clean run fish from the Lake the following year, the rivers were a major disappointment. However lovely the scenery may be there is little more depressing than spending a day heaving a minnow as far as one can into a featureless piece of still water and lake fishing quickly began to pall.

By this time the odd fish had been seen with ulcers on it and although at the time nobody realised the tragedy that was to follow it seems likely that the dread "disease" was even then beginning to show itself.

By the end of my week in Ireland in 1965 I had finally decided that it was time for a change and, together with Brassey-Gottlieb, arranged to take a really good fly beat on the Blackwater at Mallow the following spring. As I had now been working in the City for eight years and my original salary of £315 pa had increased somewhat to a level where I had a little spare cash, it seemed reasonable to spend some of this on the one thing that I really enjoyed doing in my two weeks holiday each year. The beat we chose was for four rods but, strangely, I cannot remember who else came with us. We rented a cottage with a cook and arrived expecting to catch at least a fair proportion of the 70 fish that the same beat had yielded in the same week the previous year. We were destined to be utterly and totally disappointed The previous weeks had seen very few fish landed and the banks were littered with dead and dying salmon in various stages of decay. It was the beginning of UDN.

During the week we took only two fish between us and, although I was the lucky rod on each occasion, it was little short of a disaster. It is sometimes possible to find a silver lining behind the darkest of dark clouds and even this trip had one tucked away. After years of spinning I was fly fishing again and, although I was to catch one further fish on a spinner some years later, the intense pleasure of simply casting a fly led to a determination that never again would I actually take any fishing that involved spinning or lease water where others were allowed to spin. It has been a resolution to which I have stuck firmly over the past 37 years.

I got married for the first time that summer and, very sadly, as it was a place I loved, I have never returned to Ireland since.

That is something that must be put right very soon.

CHAPTER FIVE

THE UPPER OYKEL

As this is a book about fishing with only a few other elements thrown in but is in no way an autobiography, I will pass quickly over the next few unsatisfactory years which provided me with a wife in 1966 and, later, an adopted son, of whom more later, and ended in separation and eventually divorce in 1972.

I fished very little during this time. One of the few days I did get, the year after we were married, resulted in my final fish on a spinner coming from a day on the Teith in Perthshire. This was organised by friends of my wife with whom we were staying at their lodge, Ardhuillerie, just north of Callender. I set off alone with minimal instructions as to where I was going or which pools were most likely to hold fish. As always I was intent on using a fly but when by mid afternoon nothing had moved, I switched to a spinner. This quickly raised a fresh 8½ lb fish. Playing and landing it on a spinning rod with the dreaded fixed spool reel gave me little pleasure and I am glad to say that, although I kept both rod and reel for many years to come, I never used them again except when trying to catch something in a sea loch.

By 1970 the urge to throw a fly again had become irresistible and this time I did not make a mistake. Indeed luck pointed me towards the best bit of fishing that I have ever taken and, arguably, the best fishing hotel in the British Isles. The Oykel in Sutherland had long been regarded as one of the foremost of the smaller salmon rivers of Scotland but until the late '60's only the lower half of the river, below the bridge that carries the main road from Bonar Bridge to Ullapool and the Kyle of Lochalsh, had been let or seriously marketed. At that time the Oykel Bridge Hotel had recently been built on to, with a large new two storey extension at the rear thus increasing the number of rooms available. In order to take maximum advantage of this increased capacity it was obviously sensible to let the Upper Oykel, as well as the lower

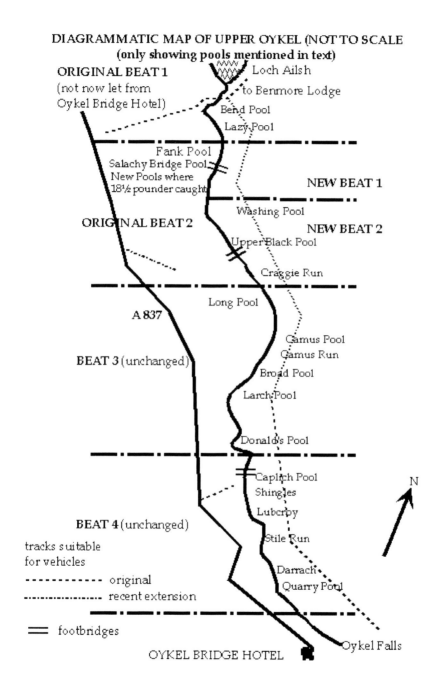

DIAGRAMMATIC MAP OF UPPER OYKEL (NOT TO SCALE
(only showing pools mentioned in text)

ORIGINAL BEAT 1
(not now let from
Oykel Bridge Hotel)

Loch Ailsh

to Benmore Lodge

Bend Pool

Lazy Pool

Fank Pool
Salachy Bridge Pool
New Pools where
18½ pounder caught

NEW BEAT 1

Washing Pool

ORIGINAL BEAT 2

NEW BEAT 2

Upper Black Pool

Craggie Run

Long Pool

A 837

Gamus Pool
Gamus Run

BEAT 3 (unchanged)

Broad Pool

Larch Pool

Donald's Pool

Caplich Pool

Shingles

Luberby

BEAT 4 (unchanged)

N

Stile Run

tracks suitable
for vehicles

Darrach

Quarry Pool

- - - - - - - original
· · · · · · · · · · · · recent extension

═══ footbridges

OYKEL BRIDGE HOTEL

Oykel Falls

river, as soon as the salmon started to jump the falls in late June or early July. As with the Lower Oykel, the upper river stretches about 7 miles and was divided into four beats offering more than adequate fishing for two rods on each beat. At the top of the upper Oykel Loch Ailsh held a reasonable stock of water, but, more importantly, its watershed, including Ben More Assynt and a large area of the surrounding hills, was huge and Ben More itself often attracted rain when other parts of Sutherland and Ross-shire remained dry.

Even thirty years ago the river was undeniably a spate stream but in those days a good downpour lasting a few hours provided adequate water to keep the whole river in good order for about three days. Solid rain on a Sunday would mean that, without further water during the week, the river was still fishable and could be expected to yield a few fish right through until the following Saturday. Most of the upper river was surrounded by young conifers that had been planted in the last year or so and once off the approved tracks the approaches to the river on foot were rough and hard going. I do not remember anyone at that time warning of the dire consequences that this forestry was to have in years to come.

Despite its ability to release water over a relatively long period, there was, even then, nothing that could be done in drought conditions and late August and early September 1970 were unrelievedly dry, hot and sunny. Once again my first view of a new river was in conditions that resembled the Sahara.

I have always maintained that fishermen as a whole are the nicest of all field sportsmen. Most people accept that the hunters are a mixed bunch, while shooters have a tendency to be a little "high falutin" or poncy on occasions. Anglers, however, are not often rushed, noisy or obscene. Their pastime does not lend itself to anything more than to gentleness and gentlemanliness. As a result I once again fell in with some charming people at the Oykel Bridge Hotel and thus, despite the weather, which rendered the fishing pointless I thoroughly enjoyed myself. We fished the river without hope for a day or two and then turned our attentions to the Loch. Still water fishing has little interest for me compared to a stream but in drought conditions it at least offers the chance of a fish while sea-trout and brown trout always seem likely to relieve the boredom by taking a salmon fly. We caught nothing but I did briefly make contact with something heavy which set off for the bottom and came off.

Perhaps it was the hotel as much as the company that made me determined to return. Just as it still does today, the Oykel Bridge had an air of relaxed comfort that put one in exactly the right mood to enjoy its wonderful food and friendly service. Both breakfast and dinner were on a help yourself basis from a sideboard running down the middle of the dining room piled high with food. There was always everything one could possibly want for breakfast, including prunes, and in addition to all the usual things that can be served with various types of eggs there was inevitably some form of fish – usually kippers or smoked haddock.

But it was dinner that really set the hotel apart from all others I have been to. Soup or some small but delicious fish dish preceded the arrival of the main course. This might consist of two enormous joints, perhaps one of beef and one of pork, or one of lamb and a couple of chickens but once a week there would be lobster and on another day a whole grouse each.

Puddings numbered four or five alternatives each night followed by cheese. Not being particular about my wine I never, in those early days, worried greatly what I was drinking but it was always adequate. Being the only thing apart from tips that got added to the bill beyond the cost of normal board and lodging plus the fishing, I impecuniously avoided much more than house wine, always following dinner with one or two Glenmorangies, for which I developed a taste.

The Upper Oykel itself, purely seen as a river, is very pretty but it flows through country that is not terribly beautiful. Apart from the dreaded forestry conifers there are few trees and the land is somewhat featureless. The river is an absolute delight. No two pools are remotely the same and from a width averaging about 20 foot just below the loch it gathers itself into something nearer three times that size by the time it has flowed down the 7 miles to the Oykel Falls just above the hotel. Every pool is ideal fly water and virtually all are easily reachable with a single handed rod and a little not very dangerous wading.

For my purposes I could not have found a better place.

It is strange that the people in with whom I have fallen when fishing have so often been ex colonial officers of one sort or another. Lawrence Boyd and his wife were another such couple. I first met them in 1970 on my initial visit to the Oykel Bridge. Charming and welcoming they were the easiest of people with whom to share a beat and by the middle of the week I was also sharing their table. They were not only also fishing the upper river but were informative and amusing company in the evenings. Odd how one can remember names from thirty years ago as if it was yesterday, while the chap one met at a dinner party last week might have been Houdini for all one can recall.

So the die was cast. I would return to the Oykel Bridge in seven out of the next nine years, five of which would be, by my standards, extremely productive, and, later, after being jocked off the river in 1981, having been unable to take up my rod in 1980, I returned again in 1993 after a thirteen year absence and continued to take a beat there until 2000. By then it was a very different place.

*   *   *

But back to my second visit in 1971. The Boyds were still there as were another couple called Cookson together with their charming daughter Mary aged about 22. I shared a beat with the former.

I was now 34 and the most salmon I had ever caught in a week had been the three fresh run fish on the Laune on a spinner. My expectations and demands were therefore not very high. However, arriving to find inadequate water yet again was not good but was this time not to prove a total disaster. It was overcast and by Monday night rain was edging in from the west and a spate seemed certain. We were not to be disappointed.

Tuesday morning saw the gauge below the new bridge outside the hotel, which I had never before seen showing a positive reading, at 3′ 6″ and the hotel was abuzz with that indefinable hurry and enthusiasm that marks the strange certainty that today is the day. The two top beats on the upper river are less suited to high water than the lower two and for this second day of the week we had beat three, perhaps the best high water beat of all. It is a long stretch, running from below Craggie Pool to a point just above the suspension bridge across Caplich. In good water it provides a considerable amount of fishing for its two rods. At that height the Long Pool, Camus Run, the Broad Pool and the Larch were all easily fishable towards the tail and enough of the water could be fished from the bank to make wading unnecessary.

My fishing book gives very sketchy details of the fish we caught that week, and I cannot remember anything about Lawrence Boyd's success or otherwise, but I have no doubt that he did least as well as I. One of the problems of salmon fishing in September is that the fish naturally tend to be red and most of them can be expected to be grilse. Small red grilse do not produce the greatest sport once hooked, but this disadvantage is countered to an extent by the fact that I was always using a single handed rod and I never found playing a fish anything but exciting. The moment of the actual take, followed a second later by the realisation that the fish is actually hooked, cannot be surpassed, while fighting it has an element of concern lest it should come off. That seems to take the edge off the pleasure. The thrill of the reel screaming or the fish jumping clear of the water are, however, times when the adrenalin flows. The salmon, normally respected and even loved as a creature of amazing gracefulness and strength in addition to having one of the most extraordinary of all life cycles, suddenly becomes an enemy that one desperately wants to defeat and see on the bank.

I had the top of the beat for the morning. It is a walk of about 400 yards from the top of Camus Pool up to Long Pool and I should probably have gone up there as it would have fished well, but I was desperate to get my fly into the water. This was the first time since 1952 that I had been faced with fishing a river designed for a fly with the water at a good height. I started at Camus. This is a small, deep holding pool with a strong narrow run in at its head after which it then turns a right angle and broadens out into a flat draw in which a number of large rocks provide excellent lies provided the water is high enough. I came to know later that larger salmon tend to like these lies at the height of water that we experienced that morning. The top of the pool was a rushing morass and far too fast either to fish or to hold a fish. In the draw I rose a fish but was unable to make it come again.

I moved down to the run below the main pool, known as Camus Run. This is a somewhat featureless stretch of water, normally only a couple of feet but on that day almost uniformly four feet deep across its breadth and down its length. I hooked and duly landed two small grilse from it The strength of the water ensured that they, only 5 and 5 ½ lbs respectively, gave me a good deal of fun. Those two hours fishing made certain that, for years to come, I spent far too much time on this run and neglected other bits of water on the beat.

At lunchtime we changed over and I had the bottom half of the beat for the afternoon. I was already thrilled with my modest success and perhaps it is against this standard that all my salmon fishing has to be judged. For the serious angler who can take expensive beats and spend five or six weeks a year on the best and larger rivers, two reddish grilse in a morning would mean little. To the impoverished city worker, who had not caught a salmon on a fly for five years, it was riches indeed.

The lower half of the beat consisted of Loop Pool, too fast and in any case seldom fished, Broad Pool which would have been at an ideal height and ought to have produced fish, the Larch and finally Donald's Pool. This last was, for some reason, deemed useless and was never fished in those days.

Only years later did its reputation change to a point where in high water it became a "certain cast" (see chapter 8).

I did not touch a fish in the Broad Pool and, strangely, have never to this day done so although it proves prolific for other people. From the Larch Pool I took another small 5 lb grilse and for the first time in my life I had landed three fish in a day. Another pointer to the sort of level at which all my fishing took place is that it took me a further five years to better this feat, and only in the bonanza year of 1995 have I ever landed five in a day!

Back at the hotel that evening all was excitement and noise again. Salmon galore were being bagged up and put in the freezer. The Lower Oykel tenants had had a field day by their own higher standards and fresh fish littered the fish house. The steaming hot water in the bath was dark peat coloured somehow giving the impression of being wonderfully relaxing and therapeutic. How depressed I get when I hear city dwellers complaining that their bath water is "horribly discoloured".

Dinner tasted even better than usual that night and the bar did wonderful business. Breakfast next day was perhaps not so greatly appreciated as on most days. A few heads were a little thick!

However, the river was still in good order and the bottom beat seems to have been disappointing. I had a nice 8½lb fish from a pool that I have down as Mary's Bottom. This was in fact the lowest run on the stretch known generally as the Shingles, a succession of lovely pools formed from ever moving shingle banks. Each year different bits seem to fish best but the last one which then gives way to the run into the Lubcroy Pool has, at least until relatively recently, always been good. It had been given its name at this time because Mary Cookson had caught a fish out of it and somewhere higher up the river was Mary's Bosom where she had also been successful. I think only the Boyds and Cooksons, in addition to me, were privy to these nick names. In later years the pool became renamed "Jenny's Pool" in a few people's minds, after my second wife landed her first ever fish there on her first morning on the river (see chapter 8).

Apart from Caplich above them, and Lubcroy below them, the Shingles always seem to be the most prolific part of the bottom beat on the upper river, but, when the river is full of fish, they can be taken anywhere along the length of this huge beat. The lower part of it can be hard work and is thus fished less often and less carefully than the top but Darrach used in the past to, and the Quarry Pool still does, hold a lot of fish when conditions are right. Still, after the previous day, this Wednesday was a bit of a comedown. To think that 48 hours earlier I would have been thinking that four fish in a week was pure heaven! All things are relative.

The next day we were back up at the top of the whole river just below Loch Ailsh. The relatively broad reaches of Lubcroy and the Quarry were exchanged for a stream on average little more than 20 ft wide. This part of the river, which included a number of charming pools, all productive with proper water in them, has sadly now been removed from the beats let from the Oykel Bridge and my memories of it are necessarily less sharp as I have not even walked down the bank for well over 20 years. A small 4 ½ lb fish from the well named Bend Pool, close to the outlet from the loch, was followed by a 6 pounder from the Still Pool, which was as badly named as the Bend Pool was well.

The final two days were blank – rather surprising as there must still have been adequate water unless there was a flood which put the river totally out of order, something that I have not noted down. Nevertheless, having never previously had more than three fish in a week during my fishing career, there was never going to be much doubt that I would return again and again to the Oykel Bridge. Indeed it became a sort of spiritual home to me over the next thirty years.

I see that all these six fish took a size 6 fly, four a Jock Scott which, together with a Thunder and Lightning slowly became firm favourites for me. If I started fishing for salmon all over again I doubt whether, even today when Ally's Shrimps and GP's are all the rage, one really needs anything apart those two traditional patterns plus the odd Stoat's Tail.

So I returned to my travail in the City and it was about this time that, in a determined effort to find something more rural in character, I tried very seriously to extract myself from a job that I had never enjoyed. I wanted to do something more in keeping with my country orientated mind. Failing to achieve this was a temporary disappointment but things were to change in the not too far distant future.

First, however, I had to get through three more fishless years. I went to Scotland in only the second of these three seasons. My divorce complicated things financially to an extent where I was unwilling to give the impression that I could afford even the modest sums involved in fishing the Oykel in those days. Things improved again soon enough because from 1975, through'76 and on into '77 I experienced the three best salmon fishing years of my life (with the exception of the quite extraordinary year of 1995 (see chapter 8).

As with most things in life one remembers the good parts best. I can recall as if it were yesterday being told on my arrival at the Oykel Bridge in September 1975 that I would be sharing a beat with a fellow called Miller-Logan who did not stay in the hotel but motored over from Ullapool every day. I have already explained that Maj Brassey-Gottlieb in Ireland and the Boyds in earlier years on the Oykel had been colonial civil servants of one sort or another and I was now to share my fishing with another. Bertie Miller-Logan turned out to be truly a nature's gentleman. He was one of the kindest, most interesting, generous and lovely men I have ever met and it was a sad day indeed when we had a letter from his daughter in January 2002 to say that her father had died suddenly of a massive heart attack a few days after returning from his latest trip to see his grandchildren in Canada. He was 90!

Although I was not yet 40 and a quick sum shows him to have been 63 at this time, Bertie and I quickly formed a deep and lasting friendship. Long after we had finished fishing together my wife and I would make an annual trip to Ullapool to have tea with him and his wife Jean in their lovely house overlooking Loch Broom, where they would talk most interestingly about a huge range of subjects. After Jean died, leaving Bertie bereft for a short time, he picked himself up and threw himself into other interests, never allowing himself to hark back openly to happier days. He used always to pride himself on making us a cake for tea! When he was found shortly after he died, he was lying by his sawbench with some newly sawn logs beside him. What a way to go!

*   *   *

For our first weeks fishing together we had good water at the start of the week followed by a flood but by Saturday night even that had run away to almost nothing. In retrospect this ought to have provided a warning of the problems to come and it may be that even in 1975 the writing, which became so clear later, was already on the wall. I started with a fish from the Shingles on the Monday followed by a blank Tuesday on the top beat. The river was stiff with fish and I could not understand why they would not take. The Lazy Pool in particular was a boiling mass of salmon, the water was perfect and it was difficult to believe that the fish were neither interested in any fly that I put over them nor appeared to be running for the loch which was a mere 200 yards away. When I met Bertie at lunch he too was blank. The afternoon followed the same pattern and I was convinced that I would get back to the hotel to find it awash with salmon and be the only guest who had not caught a fish that day.

That evening Bertie turned right at the end of the Benmore Lodge track which lead off the main road down to beat one and went home without coming to the hotel but when I arrived back, more than a little crestfallen, it was to find that nobody else had any fish from the upper river either. One or two had been caught from the Lower but with the river at the best height one could imagine the usual strange, dogmatic and varied reasons were being propounded for the bad day. Only in the morning did I hear what I am certain was the right explanation from one of the gillies.

In the night it rained in torrents, the river rose until it was almost over the top of the gauge and all day a huge brown spate roared down Strathoykel. "That's why none of us caught fish yesterday", one of the Lower Oykel gillies told me, "the fush feel the flood coming and dinna take!" It has made one of my better excuses ever since. However there is no doubt that fish are very conscious of changes in pressure.

Next day Bertie did not bother to drive over from Ullapool and I amused myself by walking down the lower river in which it was hard to determine the pools amidst the maelstrom. But it was a fine day, the storm had blown away and everyone said, as they always do, that tomorrow, always tomorrow, would be the day.

Overnight the river dropped back into its bed and cleared. It was high but fishable on the Thursday when, having missed out on beat two, we had, like 1971, beat three in perfect water. It was for me a re-run of that day four years before. I took two fish out of Camus Run and then one from the Larch. Broad Pool remained stubbornly unproductive and in those days we never even went down as far as Donalds – how many fish might we have caught had we done so in the light of what happened in later years?

On the Friday my records show that we still had "wonderful water" and I must have been very disappointed to get just one fish from the bottom beat. By Saturday, as I have said, the good water had gone but by reading Jimmy Tait's booklet about the upper river and, for once, doing what he suggested instead of pig headedly insisting on doing my own thing, I made an absolutely square cast across Craggie Run in the late evening and hooked and landed another small grilse which gave a display of aerobatics before giving itself up.

Six fish for the week was no better than I had done four years earlier but it seemed to have been a hectic week: the hotel as good as ever, the food wonderful, the company great fun and my yellow labrador bitch, Lyra, named after Julie Christie in Doctor Zhivago though for some reason always spelt differently, always enthusiastically by my side.

If 1975 had proved a good year, 1976 was even better. A simple catalogue of salmon caught is uninteresting but the overall view is far more fascinating. On the 9th, 10th and 11th of September I landed a total of nine fish myself and Bertie Miller-Logan took another eleven. Neither of us caught any on the other three days of the week. Twenty fish in a week to two rods would be regarded as bonanza time today but in the '70's it was not unusual, although it left me in an ecstatic state.

My fishing book gives, in a few words, an almost complete picture of the week:-

Sept. 9th	*High water*	*Larch Pool.*	*Dusty Miller No. 4*	*5lbs*	
Sept. 10th	*Dropping.*	*Darrach*	*"*	*5 ½ lbs*	*Missed 4 earlier*
"		*Lubcroy*	*Thunder No.6*	*7 ½ lbs"*	*Long cast, far side*
"		*Lubcroy*	*"*	*6lbs*	*Fresh run*
"		*Lubcoy*	*"*	*5 lbs*	
Sept. 11th	*Fantastic)*	*Washing Pool*	*"*	*8 lbs*	*(9 fish*
"	*day – fish)*	*Lower Stale*	*"*	*6 lbs*	*(with Bertie*
"	*moving)*	*Salachy Br*	*"*	*7 lbs*	*(Miller-*
"	*all day)*	*Lower Stale*	*"*	*5 ½ lbs*	*(Logan*

It was not to be the last day on which Bertie and I had 9 fish between us. On both occasions he outdid me! But fishing is not a competitive sport, is it? – and how different things might have looked had I hooked the four fish that came to me before I finally landed one from Lubcroy.

As always the Upper Oykel was dependent on having enough water. How we would have this rammed home to us in years to come.

Anyone who has fished this river will have realised from the fact that on 9th we were fishing beat three, on the 10th beat four and on 11th what used to be beat two, that the top beat, starting from Loch Ailsh and running down as far as the entry of the burn at the Fank Pool, had now been sold off. The hotel was at this stage letting just three instead of four beats on the Upper Oykel and this remained the position for a few years before George Ross, the fishing manager, created a number of rather good new pools and the remaining three beats were re-divided into four. In fact the stretch from Washing Pool down to Craggie Cottage, which I had always liked least of all, proved this year and the next to be most prolific for Bertie and me.

In the dog room at our home in Devon I have had for years now a faded photograph of myself holding my trusty steel rod with the equally trusty Lyra beside me. At our feet lie nine salmon and underneath is the caption:

September 7th, 1977
A.Miller-Logan   R.A.N.Reynolds
Beat 2 Upper Oykel.9 fish totalling 79 lbs
We left the river at 3.30 feeling
we could carry no more fish up the very
steep, rough track to Craggie Cottage

Bertie took this photo of me and he had its partner which I took of him in the same pose behind the same fish. I asked his daughter, after his death, whether she could locate it and said that if she did I would love to have it or a copy of it. A few weeks ago it duly arrived. I now have them side by side in the same frame. In those two shots are encapsulated the story of one days fishing in a week of success - a day that in itself had elements of farce and amusement enough to fill a lifetime of salmon fishing.

Looking back from a distance of over thirty years, it is interesting to note that the idea of carrying on fishing just for fun and returning any more fish that we might have caught, never occurred to us.

Once again my records remind me in graphic detail about the rest of the week although I need no reminding about that one day, which is etched deep in my memory. Things started well on the Monday when I took two decent fish off beat three, once again Camus Run and the Larch Pool coming up trumps. It was good to have them all on a Silver Doctor which had always been one of my father's favourite flies. Tuesday, on the bottom beat was blank – almost certainly because we had a flood – but Wednesday found us back on the new beat two which ran from Fank Pool all the way down to Craggie Run.

In those days one could not just drive comfortably up the left bank of the river along the forestry track: it ended abruptly at Broad Pool. Instead one drove up the main road as far as Craggie Cottage and set off diagonally across country aiming to end up somewhere around Upper Black Pool. Any attempt at direction finding was generally brought to nought by the fact that intervening humps in the ground meant that the river was often out of sight. More seriously, one was faced in addition by endless obstacles in the form of high deer fences and deep wide trenches between rows and rows of recently planted evergreens. In a very few years this dreadful forestry was to upset the whole eco system of Strathoykel to a point where a flood previously bringing good fishing for almost a week only gave a day before the water ran away. In 1977 ,however, the trees had not yet started to show their greedy thirst in all its awfulness.

I am only infrequently prepared to admit that the presence of a dog is a serious disadvantage but I have to say that on this occasion I could have done without having Lyra with us. The new deer fences had been installed with great care and while, by risking one's appendages at frequent intervals, one could clamber over these in places which were not designed for such antics, we could make relatively straight progress, getting a labrador under wire that had been sunk deep into the ground even where the contours made this almost impossible, was a dreadful job. In that ridiculous way dogs have, as soon as we had engineered a gap for her, through which she would have squeezed with relative ease if she had been chasing a rabbit, she refused to even try to get through it. Eventually, increasingly embarrassed by the fact that I was delaying Bertie from getting to the bank, we agreed that he should set off for the top part of the beat at Salachy Bridge while I aimed for the lower part at Upper Black Pool. I eventually arrived there already fairly worn out and not very early.

Any irritation I felt did not last long. After about twelve casts I hooked a fish in an obvious lie on the far side of the pool and duly landed it. Returning to the top I proceeded down the pool again and repeated the performance in exactly the same spot. After a short rest and a dram from my flask, the same procedure was followed again with the same result from the same lie. It would have been interesting to know how often I could have done this conjuring trick and in later years I often rued the fact that I had not continued until I fished over that piece of water without success: now, however, reminded of the story of the fisherman in heaven, who found himself forced to fish again and again for a taking trout from a single patch of water, and who after the third take pronounced "Hell!", I moved on.

I had no more fish by lunchtime and, caching the three salmon in a hole under the bank, I walked slowly upstream to meet Bertie. The bank on this part of the river has deteriorated over recent years but even then was rough in the extreme and by the time we met it was well after one o''clock. Bertie had three fish as well, all around 9 lbs which was on the large side for the Oykel. He disappeared downstream after lunch, leaving me to fish down from Salachy Bridge and meet him at the Washing Pool in the middle of the beat in mid afternoon.

At this stage neither of us had appreciated the problem that was later to face us.

I duly landed a lovely 9 lb fish from Salachy Bridge and after going down it again blank, worked my way downstream, rather disappointingly without touching anything, until Bertie appeared from below carrying two more fish. Thus far neither of us had put a fly into the usually productive Washing Pool and it was half past three. Clearly the morning had been the time and by now things had quietened down considerably. Nevertheless our next decision has seemed to me to this day to have been a strange one. Collecting together the nine fish that we had killed between us, we considered with some concern how we were going to carry them back to Craggie Cottage together with our rods and the rest of our gear. Instead of deciding to fish on and put back any more salmon that we might be lucky enough to catch, we distributed the fish into a bass and three plastic carrier bags and started on the climb up to the cars.

Today, of course, when catch and release has become part and parcel of a salmon fisherman's life, we would have taken a different view. but it honestly never occurred to us then to fish solely for the fun of hooking and playing a fish. How times change!

By the time Craggie cottage was reached 90 exhausting minutes later our action looked indisputably correct. Every time we had to negotiate our way over and Lyra's way under the deer fence, a veritable comedy act took place. Lyra became increasingly intransigent about getting under the fences; walking over the forestry ditches between the lines of new trees was almost impossible while carrying forty pounds of fish each and every time we crossed one of the fences the fish would inevitably slip out of their bags and have to be collected and re-packed. How quickly one's outlook on life can change from exhilaration at catching nine fish to frustration at the effort required to get them home.

Happily we recovered our strength and humour in time for the short photography session already mentioned. A constant reminder of the day is hardly necessary but on occasions when I feel the game of salmon fishing may not be worth the candle, that shot is there to take me back to a day that Bertie remembered until he died. I shall do so as well.

Next day I took a beautiful 12 lb fish from the tail of Camus Pool (why is it so satisfying to hook a fish in the relatively slow flat water at the draw of a pool?) and then had a further four salmon on the last day of the week. My fishing book is annotated "11 fish in the week – Miller-Logan had even more – a really superb week – good water all the time".

One week's fishing on the Upper Oykel in each of the years 1975, 1976 and 1977 had yielded me a total of 26 salmon. Those were the days – but they were not to last.

CHAPTER SIX

AU REVOIR OYKEL: HELLO GLEN STRATHFARRAR

By the standards of anyone who fishes for salmon regularly or who has access to the best rivers and best beats, by means of invitations or finance, 26 fish in three weeks is not a lot. Those of us who are less fortunate count our fish more in single figures, often regarding as a triumph anything that is not a blank year.

When I went back to my unexciting office after the week at the Oykel Bridge in 1977, therefore, it was in a somewhat euphoric state of mind. It is strange how often an excess of high or low spirits is so frequently followed by an unforeseen change of circumstances. In this instance my personal life was about to be totally transformed for the better – by the time I returned in 1978 I had re-married – but my fishing was about to hit an unexpectedly rather low point. The Upper Oykel on which I had had so much fun gave me two years of disappointment in 1978 and 1979 and after that I was not to return there for a further thirteen years.

I had never taken a woman fishing with me before but my new wife, Jenny, had fished on the Mallart, a tributary of the Naver, in her teenage days when staying at Loch Choire and on the basis of joining 'em if you cannot beat 'em, she was keen to try her hand. I had her casting on the lawn at home and by dint of tying the line to my toe and thrashing around in the swimming pool I taught her the elements of how to play a fish. Whether Jenny enjoyed fishing or not was clearly going to make a dramatic difference to the rest of my life and we travelled north to the Oykel in September 1978 with me hoping even more fervently than usual and she, on instructions, praying hard, for a wet week.

We arrived at the hotel to find the gauge showing 3 ft. The usual air of expectancy when the weather was helpful pervaded the hotel and the evening was full of optimistic chat and laughter. I told Jenny that there was no problem and we

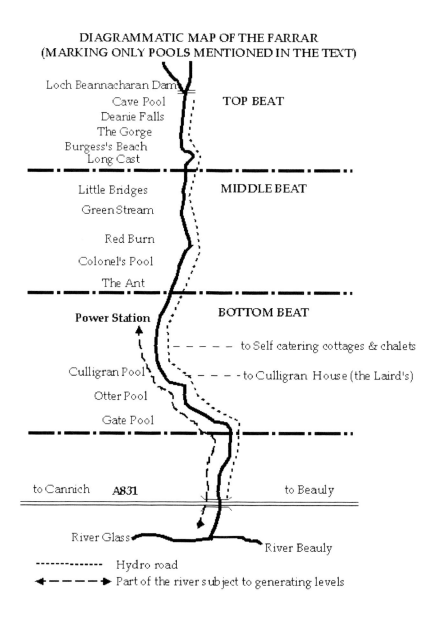

DIAGRAMMATIC MAP OF THE FARRAR
(MARKING ONLY POOLS MENTIONED IN THE TEXT)

Loch Beannacharan Dam

Cave Pool   **TOP BEAT**

Deanie Falls

The Gorge

Burgess's Beach

Long Cast

Little Bridges   **MIDDLE BEAT**

Green Stream

Red Burn

Colonel's Pool

The Ant

Power Station   **BOTTOM BEAT**

– – – – – to Self catering cottages & chalets

Culligran Pool   – – – to Culligran House (the Laird's)

Otter Pool

Gate Pool

to Cannich   **A831**   to Beauly

River Glass   River Beauly

----------- Hydro road

◄ – – – ► Part of the river subject to generating levels

would have a fish or two next day. I wished that I was as certain as I sounded.

In the morning we duly met Bertie Miller-Logan and, the necessary introductions having taken place and having agreed that we should fish the top part of beat four in the morning and swap over at lunchtime as usual, we set off for Caplich. Almost immediately I broke my old steel rod. It quite simply snapped above the centre ferrule as I cast. Disaster seemed to have struck but a quick trip back to the hotel – lucky we were not on the top of the river – extracted both the loan of a rod from Ian, the barman, and also a promise from him that he would have mine mended by that evening. We returned to the river lower down with the idea that, having lost a good deal of time, we should time things to arrive at the main holding pool of Lubcroy before we had to give way to Bertie. Almost at once I had a small grilse of 5 ½ lbs from the middle of the Shingles It was fresh, fish were showing everywhere and I really began to think that our luck was in and that a bonanza week might be in prospect.

These thoughts were in no way dispelled when, a few minutes later in the bottomost Shingles, still then known to me as Mary's Bottom, Jenny hooked her first salmon. She played it tensely at first, but, coached by me in a way that I hoped was helpful and not bossy or overbearing, it came safely to the gaff. There are a few people who get little or no thrill from the feel of a salmon taking a fly, from its strength as it runs, from the feeling that one is doing battle with it as one plays it, but they must surely be soulless and a bit odd. Jenny was not one of those strange people. She was thrilled and enthralled – she was the one that was hooked!

In retrospect I feel that it was perhaps a good thing that events now took a turn for the worse. Had we had a week of endless easy success it might have spoilt her: in fact the Oykel now turned its darkest mood on us. Despite excellent water all the week neither we nor our fellow guests could persuade them to take. From lunchtime that Monday until the late evening on Saturday neither of us touched a fish. As an example of the glorious uncertainty of field sports it was unequalled. As we drove down the track on the far side of the river that night, we stopped opposite Lubcroy.[1] As beats on the Oykel change at 6 pm there is always the chance of a cast on the beat below one's own on the way home. Jenny stayed in the car as I walked quickly down and fished the run in at the head of the big deep pool. Almost immediately I hooked a fish. I had got to that point where you begin to feel it is properly on when it promptly came off. It is an odd old game.

*   *   *

The following year my wife was heavily pregnant in September and I travelled north alone. Again the Oykel was a massive disappointment. We had perfectly adequate water for the first half of the week but I took only one 7 lb fish. At the top of the first Shingles pool I had a hard knock in the centre of the stream. I went down the rest of the run which was blank and returned to the top to try the taking fish again. The result was the same – a definite pull in the centre of the stream. Crossing to the far side I covered the fish for the third time and this time it grabbed the fly properly, and after re-crossing, with some difficulty I gaffed it safely.

And that was that – not just for the week but for fourteen long years.

In 1980 we could not take up the week we were offered at the Oykel Bridge and despite the fact that I had told them that we would definitely return in 1981, the hotel followed the strict rule that sitting tenants would be offered their lease in the next season and in 1982 we were unable to obtain a beat at all. I have long thought that this rule is applied too strictly. In the nature of things, it is always probable that on odd occasions long standing tenants will be unable for a huge variety of reasons to return year after year without a break and there is a perfectly workable alternative. If somebody who has become a regular visitor gives notice that he cannot take up his lease in any one year but can return

---

[1] at this time we were still fishing only three beats on the upper river

the next, surely it is realistic to offer his rod to someone else on the clear understanding that the offer is for that one year only? He could even be given first refusal if the original tenant turned out not to be able to return for a second year. In that case the latter would forfeit all further rights to that rod in future. Would that not be a fairer way of handling things?

In those days the Upper Oykel was so sought after that it really was a case of "dead men's shoes". Today, sadly, lack of both fish and water means that this seems to be slowly changing.

In that strange way that life has of knocking one down one moment, and then, out of the blue, picking one up the next, this "jocking off" that we suffered and complained about so bitterly, was to lead to years of pleasure in what we believe to be the most beautiful glen in Scotland.

*　　*　　*

With nowhere to go and no idea of where to look for affordable salmon fishing in 1981, I finally wrote to the fishing correspondent of "Trout and Salmon" magazine for the North East of Scotland, asking for his advice. He made a number of suggestions, which he followed closely by strictures about the unlikelihood of rods being available but ended up by saying that we could do a lot worse than approach the Glen Affric Hotel in Cannich near Beauly. They apparently had a number of beats on the Glass, which, when it was joined by the Farrar, formed the renowned Beauly itself. We duly booked a room and single rod for the end of September/early October at this hotel of which, as a result of a number of enquiries, we had heard mixed reports: on the basis of "faute de mieu" we drove to Scotland again after a gap of only one season.

As inauspicious starts to marvellous outcomes go. this was a prime example. We passed the Tay which was over its banks, a huge brown flood that was clearly to be unfishable for days to come, and the high bridge on the A9 over the Findhorn also showed that river to be a mass of foaming muddy water. My heart sank and even Jenny who was, after three years of marriage, adept at keeping my spirits up in times of adversity, began to have doubts as to whether we would get a line in the water during the week. Turning off the main road through the back of Inverness, we drove up the south side of the Beauly Firth, over Lovat Bridge and headed west for Cannich. Little of the Beauly can be seen from this road and what does come into view is mainly a loch like expanse of water above one or other of the hydro electric dams that have gone so far towards completely ruining the whole system. Thus it was not until we crossed the bridge over the Farrar, which meant nothing to us at the time, but which we were to come to know so well in the ensuing years, that the river came more often in sight. From the confluence of its tributaries at Struy, the Beauly disappears and is split into the Glass, the larger and far less interesting but more prolific of the two, and its smaller sister the Farrar. The latter, running only slightly north of west, disappears up its own glen while the Glass continues westwards arriving eventually at Glen Affric itself.

On this, the first occasion that we saw it, the Glass served only to reinforce the depression that we had felt throughout the drive north. With more rain forecast the chances of the river being fishable appeared increasingly slight as it was now over its banks the whole way to Cannich. Neither did the first sight of the hotel raise our spirits. It is about the most unsightly building one can imagine: a Stalag Luft type edifice reminding one of nothing more than a prison. Inside it is austere, comparing badly in every way with the beloved Oykel Bridge. Nevertheless we had a perfectly adequate room with a useful little ante-room area where Tamar, our new, very beautiful but rather boisterous black labrador, could sleep and ablute at will without waking us with his licking.

It was odd that having bathed and changed, we seemed, on going into the bar, to be the only guests who were not in high spirits. We soon got talking to a charming old boy called Bayley (or some such name) with his two sons, who had fished the Glass for many years. From him we learned that the river fished at its best bank high, that we needed all the rain we could get and that a good week seemed certain.

Accordingly we turned our attention to the acceptable but far from outstanding dinner, with rather more enthusiasm. (The food was to prove no more than adequate and even I, a keen pudding man, found it difficult to enjoy the stream of brightly coloured "desserts" that were offered each evening.)

Next day there was an anti climax. While the rest of the hotel set off to enjoy the Glass, we were sent to fish the Farrar. For the first time we drove up the road to the locked gate at the bottom of the fishing, found, more by good luck than good management, the beat that we were meant to be on and set about the first of what were to be so many days on this delightful little river. Elsewhere in this book there is a full description of how the Farrar works so I will content myself here with saying that, being hydroed, there is never any more water in this river than is allowed down it by the standing agreement with the electric authorities. We had a flimsy and not very clear map to guide us, but in the main fished where I thought we ought to. Doubtless we missed a number of good places and we remained blank for most of the day. Late in the afternoon, however, having by that time reached the point at which we were trying anywhere that looked even remotely likely to hold a fish, I crawled under some trees, and manouevred myself into position to fish a possible looking pot in the middle of the fast, shallow run. Casting back handed I, quite by chance, landed the fly exactly where I wanted it and the fish took at once. Jenny arrived on the scene as I landed it and we hugged each other. Strange how at times one can remember exact words years later: I said "Well it was worth coming after all!". As understatements go it was to become, although we knew nothing of it at the time, a classic.

In those days the hotel had a good deal of water on the Glass and on each of the next two days we both had two fish. It goes without saying that as hers were only the second and third of her life, Jenny was more highly delighted than a more experienced angler would have been. On the Wednesday evening she was relating to old man Bayley how twice during the day she had had a definite pull but could not get the fish to come to her again. His tip to her has since been worth many a salmon to us both. "When that happens", he said, " get out of the water, smoke a cigarette, or powder your nose and wait ten minutes. Go in again ten yards upstream and fish down again. It is a taking fish and it is even money that it will come for you again".

On the Thursday we were back on the Farrar. By now it had turned cold as well as wet and we were glad that the hydro road that runs alongside the full length of the river allowed us to park the car beside it and we dived into it at regular intervals to thaw out before wading into the river again. Cups of hot coffee at regular intervals were generously laced with whisky. The tops of the surrounding mountains were white with snow and the stags were roaring as the rut got under way. That is surely how early October in the glens should be but so rarely are today.

Bayley's instructions to Jenny were quickly put to the test. She had a solid pull from a fish in the centre of a nice looking run which we now know to be too shallow to hold fish but which must then have been deeper. Following her guru's advice to the letter, she clambered thankfully out of the cold and back into the car, downed a quick dram and waded out again. This time the fish took solidly. Another lesson well learned.

I had another fish out of the same hole from which I had taken one on the Monday, this time in even heavier, faster water as the freshet, which puts the river up by about 6 inches every Thursday and Friday, was on and our love affair with the Farrar had started. At the end of the week, despite the fact that we took three more fish from it, the Glass seemed ordinary beside the fascination of the smaller river.

However, ten fish to one rod in the week was more than enough to tempt us back and, when we returned to the Glen Affric Hotel in 1982 the water was high once more, the fish took with alacrity and we repeated our success. To three more fish off the Farrar over two days were added nine from the Glass and a dozen in total for the week, still to just one rod, seemed a wonderful return.

In 1981 I had asked for the bill at the end of the week and was presented with a demand for £247, which included full board at the hotel, VAT, our drinks, the fishing and a service charge! In 1982 it had risen to £280. As value for money goes it represented the best fishing and accommodation I have ever leased. There seemed no reason to look for anything better but we were only to return for two odd nights some years later.

Early in 1983 I was sitting in a little barber's shop in Exeter, idly looking through a travel magazine when the name Strathfarrar caught my eye in a list of places offering self catering accommodation in Scotland. This was the catalyst that lead to us spending many happy weeks in what I believe to be the most beautiful glen in Scotland. Just as I had been one of the first people to fish the Upper Oykel after the landlord started to let it in 1970, so Jenny and I became some of the earliest guests to take advantage of Frank and Juliet Spencer-Nairn's quite excellent self catering chalets and cottage in this gem of a place. Years later I wrote the following article which was duly published in "Trout and Salmon" and which I reproduce here with their permission.

WATER GUARANTEED

In the grip of a heatwave it is comforting to know that there is a river that, while not producing bonanza catches of salmon, can be relied upon to provide a fish or two when other rivers are showing their bones.

If you are an impoverished salmon fisher, in love with the Highlands, and can get away for only one week's fishing a year, where do you go? To drive hundreds of miles north only to find the spate river you have chosen virtually dry is a depressing business, while the bonanza that you may enjoy every few years is hardly enough to offset the gloom of driving south again on so many other occasions facing another 51 weeks before, all expectant, you can venture north again.

Such fishermen would do well to look towards one of the smaller hydro-fed rivers where a fishable level of water is always assured. The chance of a dozen fish in a week may be nil but at the same time the likelihood of a blank is greatly reduced.

The Farrar is just such a river. Delightfully varied throughout its fishable length, its natural source lies not far from the west coast, whence it runs slightly south of east to join the River Glass at Struy.

Today the huge Loch Monar, which has excellent trout fishing, is solidly dammed at the top of the system and another dam at the eastern end of Loch Beannacharan forms the upper limit of the fishing, which is split into three beats over seven miles.

A steady flow of water is released from this lower dam, giving a reasonably fishable level for four days each week, while on the remaining two days the flow is increased to a point where most of the pools are at an ideal height.

Of course, this is, sadly, stale water. Many of the feeder streams on the top and middle beats are also milked by the hydro and only a really solid downpour will put a worthwhile amount of fresh water into the river.

Near the bottom of the fishing, Culigran Power Station provides the one stark and unhappy contrast to the unmatched beauty of the rest of Strahfarrar, spewing forth a huge volume of water when generating is in progress and rendering most of the lower part of this beat unfishable.

Even this, however, is not without its compensations, as fresh fish seem then to be drawn into the Farrar from the Beauly and, when generating stops, a good chance of a fish exists as the water drops quickly away.

Not for the faint-hearted or stereotyped fisherman is the Farrar. The river presents an enchanting challenge to anyone who enjoys earning his fish by reading the water, and over a period of time, coming to terms with the eccentricities of the river that are caused by the varying water levels,

Anglers have cause to be thankful for the hydro road that runs the whole length of the glen. Once through the locked gate at the bottom of the fishing, there is a wonderful sense of being away from the real world and most fishermen staying in the Laird's excellent self-catering accommodation take good care to bring enough provisions to last the whole week, thus avoiding the necessity of returning to civilisation to re-stock.

The top beat runs mainly through a rocky ravine, parts of which are breathtakingly beautiful while access is far from easy. Eventually the river becomes more open and the Middle Beat starts sedately with a number of easily fished pools, before plunging into another deep cleft.

The boundary with the Bottom Beat comes some way above the power station, thus giving it some fishable water even when the generator is on, at which times the tail of Culigran Pool also gives a good chance of a fish as it enters the tail of the pool after a hectic run up through the heavy rapids below. With the generator off four or five pools below the power station give ample fishing for two rods.

Foolish is the angler who sticks to the named pools on the Farrar. This is not a river for those who want a gillie to set them in at the top of a long pool that they can fish down mechanically and with little thought.

Almost anywhere along its seven mile length a taking salmon may be lying. Often, fish trapped in a small run or deep pot by the sudden and unexpectedly fast drop in the water level caused by the end of the freshet, or by the generator being turned off, will be in a taking mood. A good deal of care is needed when wading below the power station as the water can rise two or three feet in as many minutes if generating starts and one can easily be caught in the middle of the river with no way back to the bank, or on the wrong side of the river entirely, necessitating a long walk down to the bridge at Struy or up to a crossing place above the generator.

My records show that of the fifty or so fish caught on the Farrar by me and my family over the years, about one third have come from unmarked runs or pools. The endless fascination of all these aspects of the river goes a long way towards compensating for the unnatural element that the hydro system has brought.

If the Farrar is a fascinating river, it is also a fickle one. Taking my son with us in search of his first salmon in 1989 when he was 20, we put him in all the best places, allowing him to fish first down all the best pools. He was soon to become a far better fisherman than either me or my wife and was at that time admittedly somewhat inexperienced. He fished, however, more than adequately and it was typical of salmon fishing that, despite our best endeavours on his behalf, we inexorably caught fish all round him while he remained blank.

Thankfully he returned two years later, had a fish from the Cave at the top of the Top Beat before 10 o'clock on the first morning, and followed it with a real Farrar fish two days later. Perched perilously on a narrow ledge, feet above the foaming waters of the ravine below the Ant Pool where few will have fished before him, this was a very personal success. It seemed to him that a fish just might be lying there – and it was. He will – and indeed has since – caught many bigger and better salmon, but few will be more satisfying.[1]

---

[1] Alexander Reynolds later spent two years acting as a fishing guide in Chile and became an expert trout fisherman. He now lives on the banks of the River Earn outside Perth where he teaches at Craigclowan.

In 1985, on our third visit to the river, my wife and I crossed to the far side to fish a beautiful looking but unmarked run which we later discovered was called Red Burn. In half an hour we each had a fish out of it – this from a spot that few other people then seemed to bother about. The same afternoon we each had another from the Gate Pool. Four fish in a day were almost unheard of riches from a relatively unprolific river – and indeed we have never repeated the feat. Later that same week we had a third fish from Red Burn but, until I lost one there a couple of years ago it has never yielded another to us although we have covered it religiously every time we have been there.

The Gate Pool as well, once a great favourite from which we had three fish between us in 1985, has been disappointing since then and seemed to have got shallower near the head of the pool. In 1994, however, it seemed to have deepened again on the far side and sure enough we had two fish from it as well as a 2 ½ lb cannibal trout.

Jenny has a soft spot for a small pot called Mill Stream, out of which she often manages to tease a fish.. Recently, thinking that the course of the flow had altered slightly she fished it inside out – casting down her own bank and allowing the line to be drawn to the far side by the current – and sure enough she was successful.

So the coming of the hydro may have ruined the Farrar in some ways, but in others it has created a "thinking" fisherman's river, where water is always assured, where beauty is all round you, and where, even at the end of a blank week, one is certain to have had an interesting time – if, occasionally, an infuriating one.

*   *   *

The above gives a good idea of how the Farrar system functions and makes clear that one does not return year after year to catch large numbers of fish. Indeed a week that is not blank is a successful one. It is a river where one has to search for one's fish, to take advantage of every little hole and pocket of water that might hold a grilse and above all to work hard for a moderate return. Of course there are days of excitement and endless action but more often does one find oneself returning to the chalet fishless but happy with a full day of beauty and matchless scenery in one's mind.

In 1983 the Farrar yielded us three fish, in 1985 six, in 1987 three, in 1988 five, and in 1989 six, in 1991 only one, in 1992 six, and in 1993 four. Again I have to make the point that these returns would be laughed at by those with access to good beats on top salmon rivers, but how many occasional salmon fishermen travel north each year and catch less generally in places far less lovely than Strathfarrar.

1989 really told the tale of the Farrar. We had very heavy rain on the Tuesday night and even the efforts of the hydro designers to prevent any fresh water getting into the river were thwarted. Particularly in the lower stretches the smallest burns were awash with dark but clear whisky coloured water. The fish woke up and for the next three days took more readily than I can ever remember.

It is, however, unarguable that in time the fishing on the Farrar starts to pall slightly because of its restricted size and the fact that the hydro-ed water was always the same. Thus it was that in 1993 I wrote to the Oykel Bridge Hotel asking whether they could let us have a beat on the Upper Oykel for the last three days of the season before it closed on Thursday October 1st. They could and we were back.

We returned to Strathfarrar for a week after the Oykel in 1996 and I had a small fish but even then it seemed that the fishing was less good than before. By 2000 when we started to go there again each year, the fishing was, in common with most of Scotland, disappointing – but at least there was water to fish in!

POSTSCRIPT.

While writing this in the autumn of 2003 I was interrupted by a call from a friend who goes up to stalk in Strathfarrar each year. The news he imparted was almost unbelievable. Due to an odd mixture of circumstances including a dry summer, no run of grilse in July or August, work being done on the power stations on the Beauly and a recent series of heavy downpours, the fishing on the Farrar suddenly became, for at least a week, incredibly good. One rod was reported to have landed ten fish in a day on the top beat and taken no less than twenty-one in a fortnight! It is certainly a funny old game.

CHAPTER SEVEN

CRICKET

Before I went to prep school at Woodcote House as I have related, I spent a year at a day school in St. John's Wood called Arnold House. I can recall little about it but know that we used to be put on a bus and taken to Golder's Green once or twice a week for games. I knew nothing about cricket at all and the difference between success and failure meant little to me, but one afternoon I was put to field at square leg, the ball was hit to me, I picked it up, doubtless fumblingly, and threw it underhand at the single stump visible from that position. By chance it hit the wicket and the batsman was run out. Suddenly it all meant something to me.

An interest in cricket is naturally divided into two parts: playing and spectating. Inevitably the former is by far the more satisfying and in every way leads to more amusement and the better the player the more he gets out of the game. A batsman, who scores runs fairly regularly, or a bowler called upon to perform in every match he plays, will inevitably enjoy himself more than the man who bats at eight or nine, is generally out before he has got to ten and does not bowl. The allrounder, constantly in action, who on those days when he gets a duck, may then find himself taking four or five wickets, is in the best position of all.

A love of the game itself will, however, go some way towards evening out the vicissitudes that the poorer player experiences all too often. I have never been able to understand why some people, who are poor players, enjoy their cricket, either on the field or in the stands, while others, who play most beautifully have little feeling for the game, but that is how it is.

I was at Woodcote House for only three summers. Cricket was divided into three games and inevitably I spent my first year in the bottom one. I remember achieving nothing but I must have started to think about the game in some small way because, in my second summer, and promoted to the second game, things changed very quickly. Opening the batting I scored twelve runs in the opening game and was sent up to the first game immediately. I found myself, week in and week out, playing with and against the best cricketers in the school and it suddenly dawned on me that unless things went radically wrong I would be representing the 2nd XI as soon as the school matches started. Despite the efforts of my father to try to make me take bowling more seriously, I simply was not interested in it. In retrospect this was a big mistake but, as with a lot of little boys, even the slightest pressure made me react in the other direction.

I only ever bowled in the nets and then very badly. Without ever scoring very many runs – double figures was a good score in the top game – I kept my place and played in all the 2nd XI matches that year. In only one did I make any impact. We were playing Earlywood at home and they had made a reasonable total of, probably, around 75. Although we had a solid top order we lost wickets quickly and when I came in at No. 7 we still needed about 35 to win. We quickly lost a further wicket and I was joined by Patrick Blamey, our wicketkeeper. We proceeded to create havoc amongst the opposition's fielders. We must both have been dropped three or four times and should have been run out at least twice by the length of the pitch. Somehow we scrambled the necessary runs together to win the game without losing another wicket. I was 23 not out at the end – easily my highest score ever. Despite the fact that it was completely undeserved there was a degree of adulation in the school that undoubtedly and unpleasantly, but I hope for only a short time, turned my head. At school one is always brought down to earth with a bump after such modest triumphs.

Although I did not know it at the time, the next summer was to be my last at Woodcote. I rather hoped to get into the 1st XI, but, although I played the odd match for them when two or three of their number were injured or ill, it was not to be. I was certainly not good enough. I did, nevertheless, captain the 2nd XI and this was probably a well deserved appointment as I did know more about the game than most of my peers at that age, probably as a result of the long hours I had spent spectating at Lord's, of which more anon.

Frankly we had a superb team that year. Two fastish opening bowlers who would have made the 1st XI in most years and at most schools, a wild express and a solid swing man, rather like Alec Bedser.[1] There was also a diminutive spinner to back them up. The batting was less impressive but on every occasion except one we made enough runs to deserve a reasonably easy victory. There seemed every chance that we would go through the season unbeaten. This year Earlywood caused us no problems. We dismissed them for 3! – of which one was a no ball, one was a leg bye and the single run came off our express man who forgot he had not got a mid-on and simply failed to pick up the ball rolling gently past his right hand. Fielding at extra cover near the boundary I made a bet with Mark Paterson, later the Headmaster, but at this time teaching English having just come down from University, which entailed him giving me a sweet for every run below ten that the opposition made. Sweets were the currency of the time and I duly collected seven!

I reversed the normal batting order and it was rubbing salt in the wounds when the little spinner hit the first ball of our innings for four.

A little later in the summer the inevitable but unexpected batting collapse took place and the clock was turned back to the previous year. The position was almost exactly the same against Heatherdown in 1949 as it had been against Earlywood a year earlier. Again I went in at No. 7 with plenty of runs needed. Again we lost a further wicket and again Patrick Blamey joined me. There the similarity ended. We knew a great deal more about batting this time. In contrast to the year before, neither of us gave a chance as we slowly knocked off the runs. This time the plaudits of the crowd were, I felt, a bit more deserved.

Except for this one occasion, we had never looked like being beaten throughout the year and we travelled to Eagle House for our last match fully expecting victory. We had

---

[1]George Bull, now Sir George, recently retired Chairman of Sainsbury's

dismissed them for about 35 at home after making well over 100 in our innings and any upset seemed highly unlikely. It was a hot, dry day and their ground looked a picture while the wicket was perfect. By tea we had exceeded 100 and lost only five wickets in doing so. I declared. Every one of our bowlers had an off day, they batted responsibly and solidly, not a ball moved or jumped or did anything unexpected. We didn't drop more than the odd catch that most prep school 2nd XI's would expect to do and we were easily beaten.

Once again the pedestal was knocked away.

*　　*　　*

School, as against house, cricket at Eton was appallingly badly organised specially in the lower echelons. There can be no doubt that I was no sort of cricketer by the standards of the best lower boys, but equally there were some who were worse than me and progressed further. As a result of this my cricket for the first summer at "Slough Grammar" was restricted to going in at No.11 for the Junior House Side and making no impact at any time or in any way. Due to my birthday being at the end of April, I was able to play Junior cricket for four years and can recollect nothing at all about the second of these. By the third year, however, I was captaining Wild's Juniors and, although we were not outwardly any good, we proceeded to do rather well. We had two young bowlers of some calibre, one of whom was also one of the most stylish batsman of his age I have ever seen. I had by now thrown aside any objections to bowling and was able to bowl reasonably fast and rather inaccurately but with the ability to move the ball both ways off the seam. If this sounds rather high powered it was not! I had no idea how I did it, could never determine which way the ball was going next but assume, looking back on things, that now and again it would hit the seam and inevitably alter course..

I took a few wickets and enjoyed bowling but managed to avoid the pitfall of overbowling myself. I batted at No. 5 and made a few runs – quite often into the teens with the odd twenty thrown in: this in the context of 100 generally being a winning score. I looked forward to Junior House matches, which were played on a League system, for days before each one.

The next year I was again able to slip into the Junior side and the minor successes of the previous season were repeated. Wild's got themselves into a position where they really might have won the Competition but two games that we could have won slipped away from us and yet again we were, as always, eventually just Also Rans. The one game I remember well was against Van Oss's. They were not a special side but included Viscount Chelsea who got into the XXII a year or so later as an all rounder. I bowled him off his pads and we dismissed them for about 100. As so often when it needed to succeed, our batting failed and when it started raining after tea we had lost seven wickets and still needed around 20 to win. I was not out 13 (funny how quite unimportant details stick in one's mind!) and the only other batsmen left were three virtual non starters. Next day the game was resumed on a very damp wicket. I was desperately keen to win and tried to gee these boys up to make a special effort to stay in while I farmed the bowling. Of course I was totally incapable of doing this and, in making a few more runs myself, only achieved the undesirable result of allowing my partners to face far too many balls themselves. The best non stroke I ever played was in leaving a ball from Chelsea that leapt off a length from the still damp pitch and rocketed over my centre stump. Doubtless it looked as if I was simply beaten by a good ball. In fact I know it was a case of "well left".

At this time, like all my contemporary dry bobs in M'tutor's, I was also playing for the senior House Side. We were a poor side on paper but always favourites with the uncommitted and always likely to provide a shock. Unfortunately we seldom carried a good position against a stronger side through to ultimate victory and if we did, we always made a mess of things in the next round.

In 1953 the Eton XI was captained by P.L.B.Stoddart and he had the unenviable job of forming an XI durng the ghastly polio episode which at short notice deprived him not only of his stock fast bowler but also of any supporting crowd at Lords. RDFW's Captain of the House and of the House Side that year, was a great friend of mine, Cedric Gunnery, who had also been at Woodcote House. He was a useful all round cricketer in those days and bowled fast off the wrong foot rather like Mark Proctor of South Africa and Gloucestershire did years later. In M'tutors we all expected him to be a late selection for the XI to replace the unfortunate polio victim R.James. When Peter Hill-Wood, later to be Chairman of Arsenal FC for many years, was picked in his place, we were horrified and felt that yet again the house had been badly treated. In that strange way that fate has we found ourselves due to play Stoddart's house in the House Cup a few days after the selection was made. Once again we were totally unfancied. Apart from Stoddart himself, Colquhoun's side included the XI's No.5 batsman in A. Rankin, who was also a good leg spinner and several other useful players including Stoddart's younger brother David. Having dismissed the Captain of XI for a duck and Rankin for 1, we reduced the opposition to a total of less than 100 all out and secured a useful first innings lead. When they batted again Cedric threw himself into the attack, once more determined to show that his omission from the XI was a mistake. He produced a perfect away swinger which Stoddart ma. could only edge to the wicket keeper, presenting him with a straightforward catch. He dropped it, Stoddart went on to make a century, Rankin scored 80 odd and we were easily beaten.

I have only played in a few two innings matches in my life and this was the only occasion on which I ever got a pair. I was bowled first ball by Rankin padding up in the first innings and again, second ball, in the second, this time playing a shot but not making any contact.

I have already related the story of the game against Wykes's the following year. That was really what cricket was all about at Wild's – "what might have been - if only!"

*   *   *

All this time, while I was at boarding school, my parents, and after my father's death, my mother, were living in London. Until 1953 we had either the house at 25 Devonshire Place or the flat at Harley House, both just off the Marylebone Road along which I used to walk to Baker Street and catch a no. 2 or 13 bus to get to Lord's. Provided I got off at the stop before the roundabout leading to Wellington Road the fare was a penny and to get into the ground cost sixpence. I could therefore treat myself to a threepenny ice cream during the day and still have change from the equivalent of one of todays 5p pieces. For this small sum I was rewarded by being able to watch county cricket at its post war best, many MCC matches, public schools and forces cricket and some representative games.

Now and again my father could be persuaded to get hold of tickets for a Test match and my first experience of watching Test cricket came at Lord's in 1946 when England played the Indians. I had already begun to build up a degree of hero worship for Denis Compton and when England lost their second wicket for not very many runs I told my father that we would now see something! Indeed we did! Compton, who was in the middle of an appalling run of bad form, was bowled first ball by Armanath.

County cricket in the late forties was watched by huge numbers of people from all walks of life six days a week. It was quite normal for Lord's to be full when Middlesex were playing at home and, particularly in 1947 when Compton and Edrich were carrying all before them, not only the stands would be full but spectators would be sitting six or eight deep on the grass outside the boundary boards, which were pushed in to allow extra room. Never once did I see the ground invaded by spectators. Such indiscipline would never have occurred to anyone in those more ordered days.

Throughout that wonderful summer I got up to Lord's whenever I could, desperately hoping that Middlesex would win the toss: on the shirtfront wicket at Headquarters, and with their immensely strong batting side, they would always bat first. With some impatience I would watch Robertson, that most stylish of opening batsman, and the more robust and less talented Syd Brown open the innings, generally laying a solid foundation that I hoped would not last too long. Often more than a hundred would be on the board shortly before 1 o'clock (play started at 11.30 in those days and lunch was taken at 1.30) and by the interval the Middlesex twins would have added another fifty or sixty. Their captain, Walter Robins, would demand 400 by teatime and often got it. I remember one day when by teatime both Compton and Edrich were 124 not out after the openers had put on 150 before a wicket fell.

On the rare occasions when both of these failed, one might be treated to a lovely innings by George Mann, the last Old Etonian to captain England, full of stylish drives and cuts, or a few sledgehammer blows from Robins himself or from the wicketkeeper, Compton's elder brother Leslie.

If one had to endure seeing Middlesex in the field, Laurie Gray, later a fine umpire, and Edrich would open the bowling, but very soon Jack Young would be wheeling away with his left arm spinners from the Nursery End and Jim Sims would bamboozle endless batsmen with his leg spinners that always looked so slow and innocuous. Unlike the left armers today, Young would pitch the ball, on a full length and with metronomic accuracy, on or just outside the off stump with a ring of fielders on the off-side. At worst this resulted in a string of maidens but if the ball turned at all and the batsman mistimed his drive, or failed to get right to the pitch of the ball, the cover fieldsmen or slip picked up an easy catch.

Now and again Robins would give himself a bowl or call for Denis Compton to try his Chinamen. On a good day he would defeat the best batsmen but he was never reliable enough to bowl as a regular spinner. It was as if he really couldn't be bothered with the discipline of bowling which was probably the exact truth.

When Middlesex had duly won the County Chamionship and the English batsmen with Compton and Edrich to the fore, had annihilated the South Africans, I took myself off to the Oval – a ground that I always then, and still today, look upon as vastly inferior to Lord's – to watch the Champion County v The Rest. Edrich scored 180 odd and Compton, despite having to retire for repairs to a knee, which, in future years, would cause him so many problems, raced to well over 200 before both were stumped by Godfrey Evans.

When the Rest batted Gray had both the opposition openers, Lancashire's Washbrook and Place, lbw for nought and Middlesex won by an innings.

The superiority of bat over ball made for wonderful watching and I doubt whether such a constant flow of gorgeous strokes has ever again been seen up and down the country as was the case that season.

To an extent everything that followed was an anticlimax but, as crowds dropped away, and the strokes of the 40's gave way to increasingly strokeless '50's, I continued to visit Lord's whenever possible. Occasionally I would be rewarded with glimpses of past glories as the Browns and Robinses, Manns and Grays were replaced by such as Titmus and Murray, Parfitt and Hooker. Eventually the "Twins" went as well and Lords, emptier now, became mundane again.

I was privileged to see it at its best – at least until, after the massive job rebuilding of many of its stands and a huge change in the structure of top quality cricket had been completed, it started to play host to one day finals. Of course there was inevitably the odd Test Match that could not have been bettered even by the cricket produced in those early postwar years, but they were few and far between.

*　*　*

Shortly after I left Eton my mother moved to the country and "home" became the then small village of Loxwood in West Sussex. This was a new experience for me and took some getting used to. I was working in the City, partying all week and catching a train to Horsham on Friday evenings, where I changed onto the tiny steam branch line that then chugged between Horsham and Guildford. The carriages were antiquated and the engine more so, but it duly dropped me off at Rudgwick about three miles from Loxwood.

In due course I started to drift up to the cricket ground and eventually and with a good deal of trepidation asked someone whether they were ever short of players.

Infrequently at first and then more regularly I was asked to play and slowly got to know the team and the characters in it.

Characters was the right word for in those days most village sides, even in the Home Counties, were made up of proper local people unsullied by the incomers who today dilute so many of them. They were all somewhat wary of me, as I was of them, but in 1958 I asked whether they would like me to bring a side down to play them: on the first Saturday in July that year I gathered together for the first time the team that was in due course to be known as the "Also Rans".[1]

Little did I know how much fun I, and I believe most other people who represented the side over the next ten years, were to draw from what developed as a result of this initial game.

We were blessed with a cloudless, hot summer day. We gathered at my mother's house for lunch: from the outset the rule was that only wives, of whom there were few if any at that stage, for most of the side were in their early twenties, and what I described as "properly ringed birds" by which was meant official fiancees, were allowed to join the players at this stage. My mother produced a wonderful lunch, the high spot of which was a summer pudding of such mouth watering excellence that it became a byword for this annual fixture. By the time we repaired to the ground most of us were fairly cheerful!

In the late fifties the Loxwood ground was still agricultural in nature. The pavilion was an old wooden building of rough planks and considerable character. The outfield was relatively good and the boundaries short. When the bowling was from the far end, towards the road, there was the remains of an old garage at cover point, which was immersed in thick and almost impenetrable brambles into which the ball seemed to be inexorably drawn. This caused many a long delay while both sides searched for it.

Naturally, however, it was the wicket which determined the real character of the cricket. It could only be called sporting. A score in the high seventies or eighties

---

[1] due to my initials, R.A.N.

would generally be a winning one. The Loxwood side included two or three quickish bowlers who simply had to put the ball slightly short of a length around the off stump and wait for something to happen. That it did happen virtually every ball, in my opinion rather spoilt the cricket, for luck played as great a part as skill and the joys of strokeplay were seldom to be seen.

On the rare occasions when a spinner was used, the ball would turn square though slowly. The fact that it turned at all was generally enough for the untututored batsmen who made up the lower order of most village sides. An agricultural heave across the line was often their only stroke: against the quick men this resulted, more often than not, in an air shot leaving the ball to sail harmlessly over the stumps but they did make contact now and again with a spinner. Either the ball then disappeared into the next door field, or, more frequently, produced a simple catch.

This, then, was the background to the game that we were about to play.

We fielded first in the heat of the afternoon and it at once became clear that the "gentlemen from London" had no bowlers that were good enough to even vaguely trouble the better of the village batsmen. They were incapable of keeping any sort of length and their direction was equally wayward. About once every two overs they got things right but the remaining eleven balls were regularly despatched to the boundary and the score mounted inexorably.

Loxwood's captain and their opening and best batsmen was one Charlie Smith. He was the son of the local builder and had had a trial for Sussex. The story went that he had been offered a place on the staff at Hove as an amateur wicketkeeper batsman, a situation that he could, of course, in no way afford to accept. That afternoon there never seemed any great doubt that he would score 100. Long before tea he had duly done so, the rest of his side had chipped in with 20's and 30's, we had toiled in the heat and, as the afternoon wore on, bowled more and more inaccurately and ineffectively. At the interval the score was 257 for 6.

The old locals sitting in the sun on the rustic benches beside the pavilion agreed that it was many years since so high a score had been made on the ground and loudly predicted that the visitors were in for a drubbing. I could see no reason to doubt them and though it was balm in Gilead when Charlie declared, there was nothing to relieve my depression. I was certain that we had made fools of ourselves and would never be asked to come again and I saw myself afraid to show my face anywhere near the ground in future.

For reasons that, looking back on that day, I can never understand, I asked my old school friend Nick Gold to open the batting for us. After four balls the score was 18 for one. The village fast bowler produced three balls that appeared to the spectators to be around a good length. Nick, who, and he will forgive me for saying this, was not really any sort of cricketer, despatched all three into the road over the bowlers head for six. The fourth ball was identical, Nick played an identical shot and was, inevitably, clean bowled. Almost from that moment on, with the tension relieved, there seemed little doubt that we would win. All our better batsmen, and most of them were a class or two above those normally seen at Loxwood, made runs. The faster the opposition bowlers bowled the more disdainfully were they hit around the ground: when they produced their spinner who had the ability to turn the ball both ways and could be relied upon to tie most batsmen in knots, he was met on the full and despatched without diffuclty for four or six. By twenty to seven we had won by three wickets, over 500 runs had been scored in less than fours hours play and the pin of bitter, that I had arranged to be available on the ground, was being broached.

It is no exaggeration to say that that afternoon changed my life. It will appear appallingly snobbish and patronising, when looked at from a distance of 45 years, to say that the barriers that inevitably existed in those days between myself, my team and their friends on one side and the village people on the other, were in that short space of time broken down, but that is exactly what happened. At Loxwood that afternoon friendships were formed and respect was gained, in both directions, that nothing other than sport, and particularly cricket, could have brought about.

The pin proving completely inadequate, though the gesture of its presence was an important part of the day, both teams repaired to the Onslow Arms. Here, in the public bar with sawdust on the bare boards, local bitter, still with hop leaves floating in it, was drunk in large quantities at 7d[1] a half and 1/2d[2] a pint until it was time for us to trudge up the hill to the house, bath and change before returning to dine in the smarter part of the pub. The evening became increasingly hilarious as we ate and by the time we returned to the public bar we were in a state not very different from that of most of our hosts. Until closing time we mixed freely and happily with the villagers. If they thought we were patronising sods they kept their thoughts to themselves: in itself that was some sort of recognition that we were accepted.

*　　*　　*

From that day on I played more and more for Loxwood. I became quite a reliable village batsman, going in at No.2 or No.5 and, against the moderate opposition that made up most of Loxwood's opponents in the late '50's and early '60's, I could sometimes be expected to score twenty or thirty. Even the odd forty littered the scorebook if that intangible thing called form was allied to a bit of luck.

I started to bowl orthodox left arm spinners. At least they were orthodox in as far as they were meant to pitch around the off stump and turn away towards the slips. In fact, of course, they often did not pitch at all or bounced half way down the wicket generally outside the leg stump, presenting the batsman with the easiest of boundaries that neither long leg or square leg had a chance of stopping.

There were better days. Once I took 3 for 11 for the "Also Rans" against a strong Witley (Surrey) side and was

---

[1] 3p today
[2] 6p today

rewarded by a headline in the sports pages of the Surrey Advertiser, proclaiming "Witley batting fails against Neon Reynolds". On another occasion also playing for the "Also Rans", this time against Loxwood, I took 6 for 27 – by far my best analysis ever – but that was after the stalwarts of the village side had given up playing.

They had been happy days but the club was shortly to begin to suffer a sad decline. Charlie Smith announced one day that he was not feeling well. Against his wishes I, having taken over the captaincy by then, persuaded him to turn out and batting better than he had for years, he made a wonderful century. Next week, sicker still but enthused by his success the previous Sunday, he played again and got a duck. Next day he went into hospital where I went to see him once. Already he had lost stones in weight. Less than three weeks after he had last played cricket he was dead.

With his death a great slice of its character disappeared from the Loxwood Cricket Club. Another fine player, Ronnie James, never played enthusiastically again and Harry Stanford, the secretary, never found the same pleasure as he had before in bamboozling the visiting batsmen with his so slow spinners. Alfie, who was a dwarf and who regularly turned up on the ground where, years before, he had bowled cunning spinners, and who could still be persuaded, on odd occasions, to umpire, appeared less often. Alf had once given an opposing batsman out lbw, a decision met with the unforgiveable remark that he was "Not big enough to see over the stumps" which comment Alf met, totally composedly, with the reply that "I might not be very big, but I'm big enough to send you back to the pavilion". Of the older regulars in the side only Des Howell, whose ability to down more than the odd bottle of light ale lead to his right eye being permanently almost closed from, we assumed, the pain of his constant headaches, went on playing every week.

By the time I got engaged and relinquished the captaincy that I had been proud to hold for five years, the side was unrecognisable from that with which I had started playing for the village ten years before. The old pavilion was standing forlornly unused while we racketed around in a modern concrete barn of a place without character or feeling. Worst of all the dreaded league was raising its ugly head and when I played the odd game for them in the next year or two, points were more important than pints.

How sad that proper village cricket died from that moment on.

*   *   *

Greatly encouraged by my side's first success against the village and finding that the Sunday after the Saturday of the match proved a flat point in the year, I hit upon the idea of taking five or six of the better players from my own side together with a similar number from the Loxwood team to play against Witley in Surrey. Although they were never a particularly entertaining side, the game provided another opportunity for my friends to mix with the village players. We were generally more than a match for the Witley side, especially when we were able to include people like Peter Delisle (Middlesex) or Mike Eager (Gloucestershire) who were county players. There were a few strange moments. Once their opening bat was palpably caught at the wicket before he had scored and went on to make 100. Cedric Gunnery, long time President of the Eton Ramblers, who was keeping wicket, was not amused!

Cedric had by this time turned himself into one of the best club cricketers around. He liked to open the batting, standing two or three yards out of his crease and playing nothing even vaguely resembling a defensive stroke. We once persuaded him to turn out for Loxwood against the neighbouring Hascombe. They had a quick bowler who had, earlier that season, had a trial for Surrey. By the time Cedric had hit his 50 off seventeen balls the trialist was heard to say "and he hasn't played a decent shot yet".

The "Also Rans" played about seven games in a season and often turned out an immensely strong batting side, but when my mother left Loxwood and we were all growing older, the time clearly came to call it a day. George Bull, who was the only chap in my form at Woodcote House whom I was regularly able to beat into last place, despite the fact that he was a year older than me, had always opened the bowling for us. In 1958 we reckoned he took an over to find his length, bowled well for two more, but was tired and expensive in his fourth and last. By 1969 he was ranging for three balls, on a length for the fourth but tired by the fifth and sixth. We were all playing less and less, the bowling was abysmal though the batting still had a touch of class about it, and it was time to draw a line under what had been fun times.

*   *   *

I was accorded one cricketing honour that I have always greatly treasured. Although the Eton Ramblers originally restricted their membership to those who had played for the XI and XXII, they started to open it up to other cricketers with some ability after the Great War mainly in order to have enough members to represent the club in all its multitude of fixtures up and down the country. I was very gratified to be asked to join the club but, knowing full well that my cricket was in no way up to the Ramblers' standard, I sought some clarification of the position before agreeing to the idea. I was told that for one thing there were many worse players representing the club, which was untrue, and for another that the Ramblers had always believed that the spirit of their cricket was more important than their success, which was probably true. I duly paid my annual sub of £1 (which remains the same today).

I turned out for the club relatively rarely for about five years. I chose the games with care, picking those in which the standard was not too high and the result not too important. I never had much success, but do remember taking two or three steepling catches at long on at Bryanston against the Butterflies and the Dorset Rangers. I once made 27 against Midhurst. How modest a score to regard as a success.

*   *   *

My playing days have, of course, long since faded into the past but cricket still plays a big part in my life. Since I became a member of MCC and since my second wife and I moved to Devon, Lord's has become a haven of peace amidst the hurly burly that is modern London. I go up every year to see most of the second Test and although disappointment has been my more regular diet there, there have still been moments of glorious and unexpected success for the England team at a time when, overall, their performance has been not only depressing but dreary with it.

The three day victory over the West Indies in 2000 stands out from many days of mediocrity. Fine weather, a full house at Lords with the ground looking quite lovely, and memories of what the Windies fast bowlers had done to us all too often over the past twenty years, all made the game unforgettable. First, the English fast bowlers dismissed the opposition for 52 in their second innings, a collapse started by a diving. rolling catch at third man by Darren Gough in front of the pavilion and carried on by him and Caddick, and in the later stages by Dominic Cork. Every catch was held, every decision went their way and the day ended with England needing just 182 to level the series at one all after their decisive defeat in the opening game.

In contrast to the fast action drama of the day before, the last day of the game was played out amid mounting tension. Atherton and Vaughan took England within sight of victory, scoring 40 odd apiece. Spectators were beginning to relax, to see a hint of success on the horizon after so many years when the Lord's crowd had been treated to many of the worst performances of England's dreadful sub-standard run. The drama and uncertainty returned as a clatter of wickets reduced the score to 150 for 8. Just 33 were wanted when Darren Gough joined Cork at the wicket. It seemed on recent form that once again the cup was to be dashed from England's lips, but this time things were different. A few hearty blows from Gough and a deal of solid defence from him, gave Cork the chance he needed. A hooked six into the Grand Stand at square leg off a bouncer seemed to put the matter beyond doubt and a few moments later we were all standing on the grass in front of the pavilion listening to the speeches.

(I was irritated enough by a slightly drunken yob behind me who kept shouting so that nothing that anyone said from the balcony could be heard, to turn and suggest he shut up! "Shut up yourself, you silly old man" was his rejoinder. Stupidly it rather upset me. I had never really thought before that moment that people regarded me now as an old man!)

It would be nice to write that this victory began England's climb back to at least respectability in International cricket. Sadly it was not to be. Although taking that summer's series by 3-1 including a remarkable two day win in the third Test, and despite a few moments of hope in the sub continent, their performances still remain very ordinary indeed. It seems to me that the idea of playing cricket for cricket's sake as did the old amateurs like Peter May, Colin Cowdrey and Ted Dexter, to name but few of the more recent from a hugely long line of talented batsmen stretching back to and beyond the great WG himself, has robbed English cricket of any spirit of adventure. Additionally the loss of captains of the calibre of May, Brearley and, from a bygone age, such as Percy Chapman and Tennyson, has led to this awful situation where winning at all costs seems the only thing in anyone's minds. There is no necessity for Test Matches not to be hard fought as well as reasonably well mannered. Is "sledging" just another depressing sign of the times or the result of the entry of the great god money into the game?

Coloured clothing has to be utterly deplored. It is inevitable in day/night games for reasons of visibility but why cannot both teams wear navy blue without all these flashes and stripes all over shirts and trousers which reduces a one day game to a circus carnival?

When I think back to the days of 1947 I shudder at todays antics.

1a. The author's father at the end of
the First World War.

1b. The author outside the Carnarvon
Arms Hotel, c 1947, aged 10.

2a. Woodcote House

2b. Mustians, the prison-like house in which the author started his days at Eton.

2c. Carter House, a veritable rabbit warren, but homely and very central.

3a. and b.
Twin photographs of
the author (top) and
Bertie Miller-Logan
(right) with their nine
fish off the Oykel.

4a. The author's wife fishing Lower Black Pool on her first visit to the Oykel.

4b. The Oykel showing its bones – compare this with the same stretch in plates 7b. and 8c. in good water.

5a. The Farrar could be quite rewarding on occasions: Jenny playing a fish in Culligran Pool.

5b. ... and another in Red Burn.

6a. The first side that the author took to play against the village at Loxwood in 1958. Nick Gold back row left (note brown shoes!). Mick Whitaker seated first from right.

6b. Nick Gold returning to the pavilion after hitting the first three balls for six and being bowled by the fourth.

*7a. The author about to net a fish for Jenny in Bonanza week.
Farrar in close attendance.*

7b. Big fish – small rod. "How are we going to land it?"

8c. Last chance. Alexander stands by with the grilse net. The falls are just below the holly bush.

8d. Big and red. 18½lbs.. Compare Farrar's expression with Lyra's in plates 3a. and 3b.

9a. Tug

9b. The author on the edge of Dartmoor on Beamish.

10a. Priest's Pool on the Beauly. The complications of playing a big, fresh fish hooked at "X" and keeping it clear of the posts (arrowed) can clearly be seen.

10b. Jenny's big, red fish from the Tay. The gillie may have kissed her but would not put up her photograph in the hut as the fish was "too ugly".

11a. The Rock Pool, Spey.

11b. Kinloch Hourn

*12a. New Zealand: for once the take, the strike and the camera
were perfectly co-ordinated.*

12b. One of the smaller ones: Steve with the author.

CHAPTER EIGHT

BONANZA WEEK.

Our first visit to the Oykel Bridge after the long absence of thirteen years was both interesting and a disappointment. Bertie Miller- Logan had by now given up fishing completely and having taken, as far as we knew, just one rod, we realised that we would be sharing a beat with another unknown character. This is always a time of some anxiety as you have no idea with whom you might end up fishing. That, as I have said, practically all salmon fishermen are charming, does little to reduce this concern. As we drove down the hill towards the hotel we saw a tall thin man with a beard putting up a rod. I had been brought up – entirely ridiculously – to believe that one never even looked at a fishing rod on a Sunday and my immediate reaction was that this fellow was no good and would certainly be the chap with whom we would be fishing. To add insult to injury he was wearing a pale blue sweater – in the Highlands!

Jenny was much amused by my indignation over this and before dinner we were duly introduced to Prof. Murray Harper with whom we were to share our beat: additionally the charming manager of the Hotel at that time, Mr. Blacklaw[1] said that, as Prof. Harper was on his own, he had taken the liberty of putting him at our table for dinner. It goes without saying that he was indeed the chap in the blue sweater and was one of the most charming, knowledgeable and interesting people I have met. A brain surgeon from Glasgow University, he was not only highly intelligent but had a lovely sense of humour and was a wonderful fisherman.

Since the original top beat had been sold off, four beats were now compressed into that part of the river previously covered by the lower three. There would have been enough

---

[1] Once, showing us our room on arrival and apologising for it being rather small, he said that as the hotel was not full we could have another for Lyra, our labrador. Showing us the next door room, he asked: "Will she be all right in here?"

water for two or even three rods per beat despite this, but a great deal of work had been done with a JCB to create new pools, particularly on what had now become the top and second beats.

This work, overseen by the head gillie of the Lower river, George Ross, had been done with sympathy and understanding and with tremendous knowledge of what the fish needed, and how it could be achieved in such a way that the alterations would last. As a result the top beat was provided with five good, new pools, beat two with three and even the already long beat three had one extra. All these pools held fish and had proved that they would also give them up. Learning one's way round these extra bits of fishable water was instructive.

To say that we were lucky enough to see them for the first time in low water would be misleading. We were upset to arrive to find the level off the bottom of the gauge and the whole river showing its bones. We were able as a result to see where the lies might be in the new pools if they had good water in them, but this was small compensation for three impossible days, 28th, 29th and 30th September on which date the river closed. It is true that, especially in the upper reaches, the river was stuffed with fish and my wife, relatively innocently, foul hooked one which she quickly knocked on the head. Reactions to this back at the hotel ranged from: "You should never kill a foul hooked fish" to "Well done! I'd have done the same – after all we're paying enough for the fishing!" As only two fish were taken from the whole river during the three days we were up there it seemed unlikely to destroy the stocks too desperately.

That Wednesday night it rained, and rained and rained. As we left to drive south the top of the gauge could not be seen. Field Sports!

*   *   *

1994 was better. Instead of three we had four days at the end of the season. Things started well when Jenny quickly hooked and landed a small red cock grilse in the Salachy

Bridge Pool after which I had a fresh one of 7 lbs from one of George's new pools that had at that time not been named. Fish were everywhere, the water good and there seemed every likelihood of a good few days. On the way back to the hotel in the evening we stopped at the next beat downstream which became ours at 6 pm and fished the Washing Pool for an hour. It was an all action 60 minutes. First Jenny brought a biggish fish right to the net where I (I hate nets!) made a mess of things and it disappeared at the last moment. Next I hooked and quickly lost another near the top of the pool. Just as the day seemed to be finishing on a rather sour note, Jenny had another one on near the tail and this time we killed it safely. Fishing one rod between us, a three fish day could not be called bad.

On Tuesday it rained – and rained and rained again but this time there were another two days to come before the river closed. Some people went out but the river was a bank high raging torrent. We walked the dog and read books and fumed. On Wednesday the river was still very high but fishable and we both had a small grilse out of Donald's Pool at the bottom of beat three. It was the first time I had ever fished this pool, it having always been regarded as useless in the earlier years that I fished the Upper Oykel. I have always wondered who originally propounded this myth and who exploded it.

If all looked set fair for a really good day on Thursday 30th September we were to be disappointed again. We woke to heavy rain and a blustery west wind, a rising river and a useless prospect. Thoughts of driving south early that afternoon were thrust aside when the downpour stopped at lunchtime and we immediately headed for Caplich. Already the water had dropped a foot from its high point earlier and I had a nice fresh grilse from the left bank of the pool near the tail. It took practically on the shingle inside where I was wading and was clearly nosing its way upstream well out of the main flow.

Moving down to the first pool in the Shingles I had another, this time rather red, fish which again took straight below me "on the dangle", actually amongst the taller pieces of grass that could be seen above the water.

With the clock moving inexorably on, we moved down to Lubcroy, below which the steady stretch of water leading to Stile Run was stiff with fish, but we could persuade no more to take. We called it a day with seven fish for the four days and wished the season had been just a little longer.

*   *   *

Many anglers die without ever knowing what it is like to have everything going right for them over a whole week. Some have the high spot in their fishing career early on and spend the rest of their life searching hopelessly for a repeat. Some, the really lucky ones, experience several weeks when they hook and land every fish they could ever hope to catch and they then tend to start regarding this as something of a norm. I was lucky in that my bonanza week came when I was 58, young enough to enjoy every moment of it, old enough to realise that it was most unlikely that it would ever happen to me again, but unbelievably happy to have the chance to know what it was like to have a whole six days of fun, amusement and incredible sport.

Our week on the Oykel in 1995 was, even by the standards of those who fish prolific rivers at the best time of year, amazing. My son, Alexander, was with us, we were sharing the beat with Murray as before, but through what I heard for the first time to be the "short trouser rule", by which a child of the rod holder, no matter what his age, can fish in addition to his parents, we were allowed to fish an extra rod. We thus had three rods between us: Murray naturally had one to himself while the three of us shared the remaining two.

On arrival at the hotel most of the usual crowd were there and the weather was unsettled. This was a good start but there was nothing to show that the next week was to produce a situation where we really became sated with landing fish and killing the odd one. On Monday the river was high, we had beat one which was not ideal for the conditions and Alexander was in bed with a bad cold! I walked to the very top of the beat and in the second of George's new pools missed a fish that splashed at my fly under the near bank. Remembering the previous year when it seemed that the grilse were trying to feel their way up almost on the grass, I let the next cast lie alongside the bank for a moment longer, the fish took and was duly landed. Looking back it was little more than a tiny hors d'ouevre to the main meal but at the time it seemed a miraculous start. The strange thing was that the day continued on a rather low note. Neither Jenny nor Murray touched a fish while I had two more slightly lower down the beat and both hooked close in to the nearside bank. Three fish for the day was ordinary but good. The lower beats had had rather more but nothing exceptional.

On the Tuesday Alexander rose from his bed of sickness, either recovering or strengthened by the reports of the Monday successes, the river was around 2'6" on the gauge and further fish seemed certain. Knowing, however, the vagaries of salmon fishing, added to the fact that we had beat two, not my favourite and the least productive high water beat on the river, a blank day would not have totally surprised us.

The top of the Washing Pool was too high, but the tail where there are a number of large rocks that give excellent lies in heavy water, was, strangely, blank. Moving down to Lower Allt Rugaidh, I sent my son over to the far side to fish a relatively short bit of water where the stream turns a sharp bend to the right and there is a well known lie under some bushes on that bank. He was soon into a fish which he played with considerable skill, particularly as it was often out of his sight round the curve in the river.

Next we moved on down to the three new pools created below the footbridge and above Craggie Run. Here Jenny came into the act with two fish from the second of these and I had one from the third. Somewhere we had two more in the afternoon and went home more than satisfied with six to our two rods. With the weather still uncertain and the river being kept at a fairly constant height by a series of cold, heavy showers, there seemed no reason why we should not go on catching salmon all week. The people fishing the two lower beats had already started to catch fish in prodigious numbers and a simple sum told us that, with nine fish in two days, if we kept up the same pace, we would end up with twenty-seven for the week. Suddenly, with the best two high water beats were still to come, the unthinkable seemed to be becoming a possibility.

Wednesday gave us beat three and Murray opted to take the bottom of the beat first, leaving us to work our way down to the hut at Broad Pool for lunch. For some unaccountable reason the morning was rather unsuccessful although I, fishing Camus Pool by myself, hooked a biggish fish from the lie in the tail – they're always big there - and duly managed to beach it at the top. I dislike playing fish too near the draw of any pool as I am frightened that they will make a dash for freedom downstream. I had no wish to see this one taking off for Camus Run and, as the middle of the pool provides nowhere to beach a fish, the only option was to walk it slowly upstream. It is a well known fact that if you do not touch the reel, but just walk slowly backwards upstream, a salmon will generally follow you without complaint and on this occasion it did so like a dog on a lead. A fresh 11 pounder was some recompense for an otherwise blank four hours.

Perhaps the strangest thing about this remarkable week thus far was that when we met at lunchtime after two and a half days fishing, during which the Reynolds family had landed ten fish and the other guests at the hotel had caught well over a hundred, Murray, who was by far the best and most knowledgeable fisherman of the four of us and probably amongst the two or three best on the whole river, was still blank!

After lunch that day things went into overdrive. Larch Pool produced a couple of fish and we went down to Donald's with very little knowledge of how to fish it despite our success there the previous year. We soon found out. While there were taking salmon everywhere and Alexander went across to the far bank where he had three in quick succession, there was one shortish stretch near the top of the pool that only had to be covered any old way to produce a take. Murray joined us having had his first two fish higher up and as 6 o'clock, when the beats change, drew near Jenny and I had had two fish each. The tally was beginning to grow and at the half way point in the week that Wednesday night we had landed seventeen fish to our two rods while Murray had another three.

I should make clear here that we were returning most of the smaller redder fish but the Oykel Bridge freezers were already groaning under the strain of those that people did kill. For the first and only time in my life I had stopped recording all the salmon that we were catching. At the time it seemed unimportant, though in that way that one so often does, I regret it deeply today. I only know that provided one was fishing with a fly that had some orange in it and was not too small, the fish were grabbing at it with total lack of concern as to its exact pattern.

There is little point in trying to describe Thursday's fishing. Murray retired to the hotel at lunchtime announcing, in his broad Scots accent, that it was "just slo-r-rghter!" having landed eleven fish in two hours from a short stretch just below Lubcroy Pool. Jenny had eight in the day, I had five for the first and I am sure the last time ever, and Alexander had three including his biggest for the week at 12 lbs. If I ever needed confirmation of my feeling that I would not enjoy hooking ten fish a day in Russia, this provided it. It had all become a little too easy and predictable.

For me, at least, however, the best was yet to come. It was difficult to know quite what to do to reduce the number of fish we were hooking and beaching. We had already started to use only single hooked flies and out of the box came all the old favourites from my father's day: Silver Doctors, Silver Wilkinsons, Thunder and Lightnings, Blue Charms, all of which it was lovely to be using again. But something more seemed to be called for to try and even up the odds that were so heavily stacked in our favour. On Friday and back on the top beat I tried something that I had long been wanting to do. I put up a tiny 7 ft trout rod that I had bought for my son and stepson from Woolworths when they were about six! It had cost £5! It had always cast a good line and was relaxing and comfortable to use. As we were hooking in the main smallish, reddish grilse with only the odd bigger and fresher fish thrown in, I saw little danger in this ploy.

The thread of unexpected incidents that runs through this book should perhaps have warned me of what was about to happen. Towards the bottom of one of George Ross's excellent new pools there was a lie provided by a large stone, completely submerged in high water but almost dry when the river was low. Now it was represented by no more than a large swirl just above where the water rippled down into the short run to the next pool. On reaching this lie I hooked a fish. It was immediately obvious that it was bigger than the general run of grilse that had been queuing up to be caught throughout the week. Despite a quick aerobatic display it behaved extremely well, stayed in the pool and, after cruising up and down it a couple of times, it began to tire and I was able to bring a bright, fresh hen salmon of about 12 lbs to the bank and safely release it. This should certainly have given me adequate warning that things were not running quite normally but, without thinking too long and definitely not hard enough, I returned to the top of the same pool and proceeded to fish down it again.

In exactly the same place I had a long, very slow, deep take. Instinct seems to tell one when something unusual is on the end of the line and I knew almost at once that this was a big fish. There is no point in suggesting that I played it – at least for the first fifteen minutes it played me. I had no control over it at all. It went to the head of the pool and threatened to leave it upstream: thinking better of this novel idea, it returned to the tail where it considered the advisability of going down through the rapids to the next pool. Suddenly, as if its mind was made up, it took off with the current, the reel screamed, I looked down to see only a few turns of backing left on the trout reel, which I was necessarily using with the tiny rod, and took off after it. As luck would have it the bank is completely clear on this stretch of the top beat and I was able to scramble over the uneven rocks on the riverside and catch up with the fish as it paused in the next pool. Regaining a little bit of line I was ready for its next burst for freedom towards the sea and was able to keep rather more closely in touch with it as it repeated the performance twice more.

I was now about 15 yards above a small holly bush on the bank that constituted the only obstacle to my progress downstream. While it appeared rather too high and too solid to go behind and take the line over, and while the water in front of it was certainly too deep and fast to wade round it, I would have tried the former manouevre had it been essential. Knowing, however, that just beyond that there were some falls, I determined to stand and fight where I was

At this juncture the good professor and my wife arrived by car having, from half a mile upstream, seen me running and assuming that something untoward was happening. As Jenny said "He only runs when he's playing cricket or the dogs are in danger!" The professor was carrying a wholly inappropriate grilse net and it was fast becoming clear that this was going to provide the only means of getting the fish ashore. The bank was high and the water deep underneath it. It was now that we first saw the salmon as it turned in the water on the far side of the river and Murray shouted that it had a "tail the size of a spade".

With Alexander stationed below me ready to jump in and beat the fish back upstream if it tried to run down yet again, I yelled that it was now or never, put on all the strain that I dared with Mr. Woolworth's tiny rod and heaved the salmon back across the stream. My son slipped the net under it, which promptly bent almost double, and heaved the fish on to the bank where it made a final bid for freedom. As it escaped the net – not a difficult task as it had not fitted into it in the first instance, all four of us plus Farrar, our latest labrador, fell on top of it.

It was a big, red cock and it weighed 18 ½ lbs. It had taken me just over twenty minutes to land and was the largest fish I had caught in my life.

*   *   *

After this saga we fished on quietly through the rest of Friday and Saturday morning, still hooking the odd fish from time to time, but the magic seemed to have gone out of things, the best was past, we had had our fill and at three thirty we packed up and drove south.

Fishing three rods between the four of us we had grassed no fewer than 66 fish. Murray, quite rightly and despite his slow start, had had 22, I had 18, Jenny 17 and Alexander 9. Of our 44 we had returned 26 to the river, sent three to the smoker, left one with our hosts on the way home and put 14 in the freezer. If one thing was clear to us it was that, for this wonderful bonanza, we would have to pay a heavy price. Luckily none of us knew how desperately heavy it was to be.

*   *   *

Our week on the Oykel was blighted by drought in 1996, 1997, and 1998. We neither hooked nor landed a single salmon in any of those three years. In 1999 we did have rain, there were fish in the river and for at least three days it was at a perfectly acceptable height. On the first morning I landed a small red grilse and released it, certain that it was to be the first of a fair number. It was the last any of us touched that week. On the Saturday we packed sadly and got on the road to Bonar Bridge. Before we got there we had decided that enough was enough and that we would give up our beat next season. I shall go back – in fact as I write this in June 2002 I have an invitation to go there this September but am considering it with very mixed feelings.[1]

I know full well that no bonanza week will be repeated and would love just three or four days of good water to feel the line in the water there again, but dread arriving in Sahara-like conditions and looking at the sorry sight of the river down to its bare bones again. We shall see!

---

[1] There was water for a day and a half: the river was full of fish but they were just running for the loch. I luckily had one of the few fish taken from the Upper river that week. It turned out to be the only salmon, as opposed to grilse, caught above the falls in the whole of September. I put it back.

CHAPTER NINE

HERE AND THERE

It was lucky that, during this period of complete drought and lack of fish on the Oykel, we were either invited or arranged to fish now and again in a number of different places and on a number of different rivers. Going to new beats is always exciting and trying to read new water is one of the most fascinating parts of salmon fishing. Indeed it is a part at which I have always regarded myself as rather good. Obviously it is helpful to be told by a gillie or someone who knows the river that this is a good pool and that one, despite looking wonderful, is quite useless, but my experience over the years has been that to follow one's own intuition about lies is generally more rewarding, especially on smaller rivers. Certainly a fish taken from a place that other people seldom fish brings a degree of rather unpleasant self-satisfaction not to be had from hooking one in a pool that everyone else fishes as well.

Much earlier, however, in 1986, nine years before the Oykel bonanza, my old friend Tony Drake and I went off for a week on the Cawdor water of the Findhorn. We rented a cottage on the estate which was a strange mixture of adequacy and appalling lack of even the most basic necessities. I understand that they have since been completely done up and are now charming and very fully equipped but that the estate maintains a certain reluctance to accept dogs. I hate fishing without my dog or dogs as does Tony, who always has a huge number of pale yellow labradors in tow, and this has, thus far, always prevented me from returning.

The Drynachan water of the Findhorn is, however, absolutely delightful. The top beat needs a good deal of water, which we did not have, but the lower two are full of relatively shallow, streamy pools, which fished excellently in quite low water and were stuffed with fish. The whole set up was badly run in those days and we were not only not told where to go but were not provided with any sort of map or instructions as to which beat we were to fish. The result of all this was that we fished the top and rather sultry unsatisfactory beat for half the week and had the lower water only on the remaining three days. That, after losing three or four fish, we finally killed seven between us was therefore pretty acceptable. I remember hooking and playing for about twenty minutes, a big fish of about 15 lbs that I simply could not manage to bring to the gaff. I was fishing a fast pool of shallow water interspersed with largish rocks, mostly half in and half out of the water. Every time I got it within reach the salmon simply lay on the current and floated downstream. Had I turned myself round and beached it, as I would have known how to do today in these "catch and release" times, disaster would probably have been averted. In the event the hook finally pulled out and a good fish was unnecessarily lost.

By Friday lunchtime Tony had had three good fish and I had one but, in that way that salmon fishing so often turns out, I then landed three in the last twenty four hours including a very fresh and strong 14 pounder.

It is a fine bit of water that I would recommend to anyone. We had an enjoyable week together despite the vagaries of the estate.

*   *   *

In 1989, with my daughter then aged ten, we searched for somewhere where we could have a family holiday at the same time as getting some worthwhile fishing. This was not easy to find but we eventually came up with Lochaline on the west coast of Argyll opposite Mull. I cannot say that, as a fishing trip, it was a major success although I caught a nice seatrout in the pool that one could practically reach with a long cast out of the window of the cottage in which we were staying. However, we did go back a year later with some friends and, after a spate, I infuriated my wife by hooking a salmon from a lie that she had just covered from the opposite side of the small river White Glen. This was something of a success as both Susie and the children of the other two families with whom we were staying were on the scene and the fish was kind enough both to stay on and to put up a good rather long range fight. This forced me to land it well below where it was hooked, thus giving them all a good idea of what salmon fishing was all about.

In 1991 we returned again but were short of water. Jenny however, in the way that she has of achieving the unlikely, had a very fresh grilse of 4 ½ lbs from Big Pool and thus the journey was not totally in vain.

The river, which was quite interesting in high water but had no great run of fish, had one fascinating feature. The White Glen, the main tributary of the River Aline, ran down into the main river just below Loch Arienas. In high water, until the Loch filled up, most of the water coming down White Glen ran literally up the Aline to help fill the loch and there was thus a stretch of the river which proceeded to run in the wrong direction. As soon as either the loch filled or the water in the White Glen dropped, things returned to normal.

Lochaline itself, on the Morvern peninsula, has little to offer, but the huge Victorian Ardtornish House that forms the basis of the estate was rather wonderful in an outdated sort of way. We twice rented the Billiard Room flat which, apart from huge bedrooms and bathrooms, consisted entirely of the gigantic billiards room in which we all ate, read and played. It had an enormous fireplace which ate coal at a prodigious rate. A whole scuttle could easily disappear almost without trace. Unfortunately one of our guests made the mistake of throwing a full bucket into a strange recess behind and above the grate, which action resulted in the chimney being set on fire. To the delight of almost everyone, we were able to stand in the garden and watch a wonderful firework display coming out of the Elizabethan style chimney pot. As the nearest fire brigade was some 50 miles away in Fort William and any fire engine sent to the peninsula was faced with either a long roundabout journey or the additional hazard of having to use the ferry to get to us, discussion as to whether we should call them was short and decisively negative. We threw a pound or two of salt on the fire instead which eventually had the desired result. The children thought it a wonderful place. One day we walked them up to a trout loch about three miles away. While we were fiddling with the boat one of them apparently fell in off a rock on which he had been standing. In the way that children have, they closed ranks quietly against us and the unfortunate boy had no alternative but to walk home and change. We only later learned that he had been pushed. It was, in fact, all of eight years later that his elder sister admitted that she had been the culprit - by then it was a bit late to beat her as she was eighteen! Although, on second thoughts perhaps next time I see her..............![1]

The main attraction of the whole place was really the garden which was still kept up as far as was possible in the late twentieth century. Sadly there were obvious areas that had become neglected but the trees, shrubs and plants in this temperate part of the Highlands were interesting to anyone with any knowledge of horticulture.

*   *   *

Shortly after we met Murray Harper on the Oykel, he very kindly asked us to have a day on the Tay each year, until he gave up his beat in despair when that river went downhill so badly at the end of the nineties. The Glendelvine beat includes the famous Boat Pool where Miss Ballantyne caught the largest salmon ever taken on a rod and line in Britain. The "Bargy Stone" opposite which the fish took is perhaps the best known lie in Scotland and as one fishes past it one always feels that another monster could be lurking there. I cannot say that the day we had there each year for six seasons was ever very productive, but we were unlucky and could well have done better. I personally touched, but failed to hook properly, three fish during those years while Jenny was only slightly more successful.

In 1994 she crossed the Caputh bridge to fish the Boat Pool from the right bank. Within a short time she was into a fish. I called across to her to ask whether she wanted help but was met with the reply that she was OK, had a net (not in my

---

[1] I promised to mention her in this book – her name is Henrietta Pinkham.

opinion likely to improve her chances of landing it!) and that it was quite small anyway. When ten minutes later she was still playing it and had not had so much as a glimpse of it, I began to think that it was bigger than she had originally expected: I thus crossed the bridge with Murray at my side and we made our way down to the bank where the salmon was obstinately and seemingly solidly deep down in the water, albeit only ten yards from the bank. Encouraged by our presence to put a bit more pressure on, Jenny managed to winch it higher up in the water and we saw what certainly seemed a large fish, which quickly capitulated and came to the net. (For once I had to admit that the dreaded net was helpful!) It was red, horrible looking and weighed 20 lbs. It was at the time and remains today very comfortably the largest fish she has caught.

So pleased was the gillie, Dave Brown, that he hugged Jenny and kissed her! I thought of my mother turning uneasily in her grave at the mere idea of a gillie kissing his client, but spontaneous actions like that seem to me to be quite excellent. Very sadly Dave got cancer shortly afterwards and never gillied for us again. He was a lovely, knowledgeable, gentle man for whom, in the very short time that we knew him, we came to have deep respect.

We had some lovely days on the banks of this famous river but only one other really interesting moment. Jenny was fishing just above the Boat Pool proper, in the fast water that leads into the head of the pool, where, for a short stretch, the flow slackens and there is a well known lie. She was wading well out in the river about knee height, but in that strength of water any movement had to be made slowly and deliberately. It was typical that at this juncture a big fish took. It simply made for the North Sea. Without stopping it stripped off her line and 150 yards of backing and the result was inevitable. Lack of experience may have contributed in some slight way to this disaster – perhaps she might have increased the pressure on the line slightly or let it go completely slack or even tried to move downstream a little – but in truth there was little to be done except rue the fact that so obviously big a fish had taken just where it did.

With the Tay so clearly short of fish, I was disappointed that people were still throwing spoons and minnows into this famous river and some seemed happy to sit all day in the boat harling[1]. A sad commentary at a time when stocks were being reduced so fast. It was lovely to have a chance to fish the Tay but I never got used to or enjoyed the great open spaces of its water and the slightly characterless pools.

*　　*　　*

In 1998 my wife's eldest niece got married in Aberdeenshire. By a strange quirk of fortune, she married the eldest son of some great friends of ours in Devon and we duly hatched a plan to take a cottage and fish for a few days on the Don. I cannot say that this river grabbed me a great deal: people were said to be catching fish lower down it on spinners but there was no sign of a fish on our stretch further up. The whole stay was made memorable by a couple of days we had on the famous Birse beat of the Dee, courtesy of a great friend of our own friends, Peter and Carol Cameron. The fishing itself was not wonderful and although my son lost a decent fish, the only other reward we had was a lovely fresh run salmon of 8 lbs that I took from a pool called The Lummels. The Dee was near its nadir at this time and we felt lucky to have made contact at all.

We have, however, often dined out on the story of the dinner to which our host very kindly invited us at his Aberdeenshire Victorian castle. We were met on arrival by the aged butler, who had originally been valet to our host's father, and who was a real stage character. Standing at the top of the steps up to the front door and before issuing any words of welcome, he demanded to know "Whair's the flusk?" Taken somewhat aback, it was a moment or two before the Camerons realised that he was referring to a thermos flask that had gone missing at lunchtime.

---

[1] Trolling lines out of the back of the boat while the gillie manoeuvres it back and forth across the river.

When we had recovered from our giggles over this, we were given a delicious dinner but, as it went on, said butler poured more and more of the excellent claret on to the table rather than into our glasses and it was clear that, behind the scenes, he was enjoying it as much as we were. When we got to the port, the girls were amazed not to be offered any. This did not surprise me as I knew it to be quite normal practice in any number of houses in what, for want of a better expression, I will call the higher echelons of society.

It reminded me of a story my mother often told of how, when she was staying with my father in a rather grand house in Yorkshire before the war, the ladies were not given cream to go with their pudding. In its silver jug, it was solemnly offered to the gentleman by the butler, who missed out each of the ladies, including, of course, the hostess.

*   *   *

Later in the same year a kind friend invited my wife and I to fish the Brae Water of the Spey for a few days in September and the beat included the Rock Pool. I was, to put it mildly, terribly excited at the prospect of returning to fish a piece of water that had such wonderful memories for me.

We had been staying the previous night at a lodge on the west coast of Inverness, Kinloch Hourn. This was, and indeed is, a remarkable place. Built at the head of the sea loch from which it takes its name, it is surrounded by towering mountains that reach up to 3000 ft seemingly straight out of the water and if the sun shines there is no more beautiful place. When I first knew it, it had no mains electricity and only the kitchen area got power from a small generator. Midway through dinner the old retainer would appear bearing Tilly oil lamps and one went up to bed by candlelight.

At that time sea trout came into the small river Hourn in reasonable numbers and one could, and I did from time to time, catch a few of them as they came in off the tide. There were also a fair number of the oddly and sadly named slob trout, which lived in the estuary. If there was a real spate these would take rather well and one could have two or three in a short time before the tide became too high or too low – I forget which! Sadly, and after a long fight, the new pylons taking electricity to Skye were routed straight across the top of the hill behind the lodge and, not unnaturally, the owner took advantage of this to insist that the lodge be supplied with power off the mains. Doubtless this was a sensible and sound commercial decision, but for me a lot of the magic of Kinloch Hourn went when the Tilly lamps disappeared.

Coincidentally, at about the same time, the riparian owner on the south side of the river went ahead with some "improvements" to the few worthwhile pools. These consisted of getting a digger in and moving a lot of the rocks and shingle. Unfortunately he failed to take proper advice and lacked the necessary knowledge himself to do the job properly. The result was disaster. The one really good pool was completely destroyed and the river ceased to be in any way viable. Partly as a result of this and partly due to the swift decline of sea trout up and down the west coast of Scotland that took place at about this time, the fishing became totally useless.

Having left the lodge in torrential rain, which followed us as we drove east towards the Spey, we arrived beside the river at about 11 o'clock and our host put me into the Rock at once. Within a short time I was into a fish. Twenty minutes later the gillie slipped his net under a 20 pounder!

I would love to write that it was a sea liced cock, taken from the same lie out of which I had hooked my big fish 46 years and twelve days earlier, and that I was using the same rod. That would be stretching author's licence too far! It was a cock but rather red and although it did come from roughly the same part of the pool the Rock has changed almost beyond recognition over the years. It did, however, take a Thunder and Lightning size 4, a rather mediocre treble hooked affair compared to the beautiful fully dressed single hook Thunder that had lured the earlier fish and while the 10 ft steel rod that I used in 1952 lasted only until the late 70's, and the line, of course, has long since and often been replaced, the gunmetal reel by Malloch's of Perth was the same one with which I had caught that 17 lb fish so long ago.

Sadly the river then rose and went out of order for most of the rest of our stay. Just rarely, however, things, in some strange way, do go according to the script in one's mind and, for me, the long awaited return to the Rock, culminating in my biggest ever fish was a wonderful and unforgettable moment. I hope my parents were sitting together on their cloud, looking down. They would certainly have been smiling!

*   *   *

After so many years fishing the Farrar and to a lesser extent the Glass, and having driven up its banks so often and annually visited the fish lift in the Aigas Dam, which opens to the public twice a day, it was wonderful to eventually get a chance to fish the Beauly itself in 2002. The nearest we had come to this before was when we fished the Junction Pool from the Farrar and may possibly have very slightly poached the Beauly water.

In 1999 James and Mary Holt bravely walked from Land's End to John O'Groats in aid of the Countryside Alliance. We were contacted by a friend of ours, who was organising the section of this epic effort that took them across the Cornish border to a spot about six miles west of our home at Bridestowe near Okehampton. We were asked if we could walk with them for a short way and have them and their back-up team to stay for the night. We were, of course, delighted to help and, even before meeting him, I had an inkling that James and I could have been at Eton together. As soon as we set eyes on each other we recognised each other at once despite having not seen one another for forty-five years. We had a hilarious evening reminiscing, drinking some of our rather moderate wine followed by a good deal of James's very good stuff.

We were appalled when, next day, they set off on the next part of the walk in pouring rain with totally inadequate waterproofs and, we thought, improper footwear. We quietly bet that they would never make it up the length of the country, partly because Mary had Parkinson's Disease. We severely underestimated their courage. Not only did they, of course, achieve their object, but in doing so they raised a huge sum for the CA at a time when it desperately needed every penny it could get hold of to fight New Labour's attack on Field Sports. Unreal! The following year we were more than a little surprised to get an invitation to join them to fish for three days on the Beauly in June, but were forced to refuse. Last year (2002) the invitation was repeated and we accepted with more than a little alacrity.

* * *

By this time my son was teaching at a prep school in Perth and on arriving there we found the Earn and the Tay 3-4 ft above their normal summer level and virtually unfishable. We were greatly encouraged by this as, if the Beauly was in the same state, we thought we might be in luck. As we knew the Glass fished best when bank high and had no reason to think the the Beauly would be any different. Slight unease crept in when, while lunching at a smart new restaurant in Pitlochry, we spoke to a girl who had just been cooking for a week for a house party on the Naver. She said that it had been a disaster and that this prime and very expensive week on possibly the best salmon river in the U.K. had yielded just ten fish due to an acute shortage of water.

As we drove on north, however, we were amazed, in this wettest of summers, to see first the Dulnain at Carr Bridge and then the Findhorn, as we crossed it on the A9, virtually empty, and when we looked at the Beauly that evening it was certainly no raging torrent.

It is worth at this point describing briefly how the Beauly fishing works. It is, of course, hydro-ed and thus is assured of a minimum level of water known as the compensation level. This, as on the Farrar, however, comes out of the bottom of the dam and is therefore stale: it is certainly better than nothing but has none of the enlivening qualities that salmon find in fresh rain water. As already outlined, the Farrar and the Glass join to form the Beauly at the Junction Pool and the stretch from there to Aigas Dam, a matter of about five miles, forms the Upper Beauly divided into two beats. The middle section of the river between the Aigas and Kilmorack Dams is fished very little, being mainly a still lochlike mass of water and then, below Kilmorack Dam, the Lower and most sought after water starts and forms three beats ending in the tidal water just above Lovat Bridge on the old A9. Very few fish had been counted through Aigas and therefore our fishing was necessarily concentrated on the lower river. Each beat caters for five rods and provides wonderful water of varied types, widths and speeds.

A short description of our first two days fishing will suffice. It did not set any records, although on the top beat the Glide just above the bridge came alive after dinner on the Monday as a small run of grilse appeared and for an hour fish were showing everywhere. Unfortunately there is no way for anglers to get under the bridge with a fish on and this had lead to the loss of one earlier in the day and now resulted in two more coming off as people tried desperately to prevent them running straight downstream and disappearing into the Ferry Pool below. The result at the end of day one was thus unimpressive – two grilse caught and three lost!

Day two was worse. Remembering the advice we had been given by the old fellow at the Glen Affric Hotel twenty years before, after I had had a "knock" in the Silver Run I went back over the fish again and it took. There was no problem landing a 5lb sea liced grilse destined, as Willie Matheson, the fishing manager and gillie, told me, for the Farrar – the gillies can tell from the shape of the fish from which branch of the system each fish comes. In the late afternoon Jenny did exactly the same thing but hers, hooked again at the second attempt and in virtually the same place, came off.

Another fish was lost on Wednesday morning and at 4 pm on the third day of our three, the whole party had caught only three fish and lost five. As things so often do in Field Sports, however, things were about to change with a vengeance.

As we were due to dine in Strathfarrar and stay the night there with the Spencer-Nairns, we could not fish after dinner as the rest of the party planned to do and we therefore kept gently at it through the afternoon with the river to ourselves except for Gordon Max-Muller who seldom left it. We first fished the top half of the beat while Gordon went down to the Priest's Pool just above Lovat Bridge. Remaining fishless we drifted down there at teatime only to meet him, equally unsuccessful, returning to the hut in the middle of the beat. Leaving Jenny on the left bank I crossed the river by the bridge, walked up the right bank and waded out at the top of the pool where a wide stretch of fast popply water, about 30" deep, slowly narrows, deepens and slows as it enters the main part of the pool. On the basis that grilse will lie in anything and that fish, having just come into the fresh water off the recent tide, might be making their way up the somewhat less heavy water out of the main stream in the middle of the river, I started well up and cast to both sides as I moved down towards the pool proper. It was one of the loveliest bits of water I have ever fished and it was no surprise to me when I hooked a fish well below me just before the fly came onto "the dangle".

Unlike the grilse with which we had made contact earlier, this was a heavy solid take, stripping off 20 yards of line in a flash. Putting this down to the strength of the water I thought little about it and refused Jenny's offer to rush across to me with the net: there being no good place to beach a fish, I nevertheless thought that I could wrestle a grilse onto the reedy, low bank without too much trouble. I had by now backed towards the bank and the fish returned upstream without trouble. As it got level with me I put on some side strain and it ran upstream above me and jumped. I nearly fell over with surprise and excitement as it was immediately apparent that far from being a grilse this was a large, fresh salmon. Accepting Jenny's renewed offer to come and help me, made as soon as she saw the size of what I was into, I settled down to play the fish and suddenly remembered that the previous day Willie had replaced my 15 lb nylon with 8 lb to make the fly swim better in the slower water on the middle beat. As the meaning of this filtered slowly into my mind the salmon made the first of two runs downstream well onto the backing. The situation was not improved by the fact that down the centre of the river, to the right of the main stream but between the fast, deep water and me, were a line of piles left over from a netting station dating from an earlier age.

Clearly if the fish got round one of these it would be gone and I therefore retraced my steps towards the middle of the river with the vague plan of giving myself an angle to prevent it moving between the piles, (see plate 10a), while at the same time trying to prevent it getting down as far as them.

Somehow I achieved this last aim on both occasions that the backing appeared and, feeling that I now had enough control over things to stop it running so far down again, I recommenced my slow backwards wade towards the right bank. By the time Jenny finally appeared with the net things were indeed roughly under control and she eventually netted a fresh run fish that looked to us to be around 20 lbs. It turned out to be only 15 which still surprises me today. All this goes to show that a single handed rod and 8 lb nylon is perfectly adequate for even quite large fish.

Having had two fish for the three days myself and Jenny still being blank I insisted that she came over to the right bank herself and having dumped the fish back at the hut, I went into Beauly to buy some whisky as a present for our hosts that evening. On my return I saw Gordon Max Muller just netting a grilse for my wife, having himself scooted very, very kindly over the bridge to help her. He had just returned to the left bank and started fishing again when there was a further scream from Jenny's reel and she was into another one. This time I rushed across and jumped into the river to her aid, unfortunately forgetting that I had removed my waders before I went into the town. All in all it was not a very professional performance but the fish was again safely netted and she was looking at a matched pair of perfect 5 ½ lb sea liced grilse – both the proverbial bars of silver.

It was somewhat embarrassing that of the six fish landed in those three days to five rods we had four of them between us and even worse was the fact that in the next three days the party landed no more at all. It all goes to re-confirm the oldest adage of all – it is pure luck if you happen to be in the right place at the right time: and I can put up with the embarrassment.

.

*   *   *

This year the Holts asked us back again, this time for the whole week. Sadly the results were no better. The Beauly was short of fish, the grilse run had not yet appeared and we worked hard for little reward. Jenny got another small grilse at 10.45 in the evening after fishing hard throughout all of one day and other members of the party took the odd fish. My week, however, was obstinately blank except for a magical twenty minutes on the upper part of the river above the Aigas Dam.

No fish had been taken up there earlier in the season and I therefore fished the Bank Pool with little hope and even less expectation. In the event I quickly landed not just one but two fish of 9 lbs and 8 lbs respectively. We had been asked to return the second salmon we caught, as opposed to grilse, all of which we were allowed to kill. I therefore had no qualms about beaching the first of these unexpected fish, knocking it on the head as much because I was doubtful if anyone would believe me if I released the evidence of my success as for any other reason. The second, however, was a different matter. It was fresher than the first larger one and fought harder. After it had taken me out to the backing and across the stream to the far side of the pool, it duly returned belly up! I took the view that it was "D.O.A." or at least unlikely to survive and kept it as well, though not without some misgivings.

While playing both fish I had been yelling for my wife and the gillie, who had gone to fish another pool further upstream, to bring me the net, but they had heard nothing. Hugh Matheson, Willie's father, nearly fell over with surprise when he saw me walking back to the hut carrying not one but two fish! His surprise was mirrored on the faces of the rest of the party when we joined then on the Lower river for lunch a few minutes later. Not for the first time I felt that the Beauly had caused me some embarrassment.

It was a dreadful year for the whole of the Beauly system - at least until very late in the season. The Upper river had no more than my two fish for June, only seven in July and twelve in August. I am, as I write still waiting to hear how it fared at the time when the Farrar became so suddenly and dramatically full of fish in October.

It came as something of a relief that, during the lean years on the Oykel and Farrar, where we have recently done most of our annual fishing, I was very lucky on the occasions when we were asked to the Spey, Dee and Beauly in quick succession. Not so Jenny who failed to score from the end of the bonanza year of 1995 on the Oykel until she took a tiny grilse from the Farrar in 2001, although she did hook and lose a big fish on the Deveron when we once had a day there.

It was therefore with more than a modicum of relief that I saw her land her two fish on the Beauly a year ago and feel sure that enthusiasm, which had in truth never really waned, was well and truly rekindled in her.

*   *   *

As I have never either stalked or shot seriously I have never had a chance of getting the legendary McNab.[1] I have, however, always been fascinated by the possibility of a "fishing McNab". People interpret this is a number of different ways but it seems that it is generally taken to mean catching a salmon from three different river systems on three successive days. It was during this time that I had the opportunity to achieve this but in fact never got over the first hurdle. Getting more unsteady on my feet as the years started to advance, I was by the middle nineties, always using a wading stick. This, however, did not prevent me falling in with increasing regularity. My son suggested a new sort of McNab, to be known as a McNugget, which was to be earned by anyone who fell into a different river on three successive

---

[1] Shooting a brace of grouse, killing a stag and catching a salmon on the same day.

days fishing. This I found an easier target. I duly immersed myself in the Tay on a Friday, had no trouble in falling into the Glass on Saturday but was let down by, of all places, the Farrar where I remained dry until the following Thursday. I have no wish to try again but do now wear a safety waistcoat on all the bigger rivers. It is so inconvenient for ones fellow guests if they have to leave the river to cope with a death – it would always inevitably be just when the water was perfect.

CHAPTER TEN

HUNTING AND THINGS EQUESTRIAN

When Jenny and I married in 1978, it was only a short time before we decided to move from Sussex to Devon. The catalyst in this decision took place one Monday morning after we had got off the overnight motorail at Kensington. We drove home against the flow of rush hour traffic, passing hundreds and hundreds of little pallid, waxen faced people sitting at traffic lights in their little tin boxes. After the pleasures of the Highlands, the pointlessness of my life commuting to Croydon, day after day, week after week, for another twenty five years, was heightened to the point where our minds were quickly made up to take a plunge into the unknown.

We wanted to go somewhere where we could ride together, fish together and Jenny could get some sailing, which has always been and remains her first love. Before we met I had taken myself off to Devon for the odd weekend, to fish or ride on Dartmoor. I used to go out from Skaigh Stables which was run by a very eccentric Irishman named David Moore, who had bred the famous Cornishman V, and by Rosemary Hooley, whose former husband had been a well known Master of the Mid-Devon Hunt. David had a hate for incompetent riders, particularly if he thought they had bad hands and he would often send these poor people out on to the wide expanses of the moor on a horse equipped with only a drop noseband and a pair of reins. If his hot temper was caused partly by the pain of increasing ill health, his dislike of all Germans doubtless stemmed from a hard war. If any of them came to stay for a riding holiday, they had to expect a difficult time from him. He was convinced that no Germans could ride properly and were only any good at dressage. He would thus take them to the top of a steep hill above Taw Marsh and say "Now, we always canter down here". If they were still in the saddle at the bottom of the hill, he would grudgingly admit that they were not so bad. However he was once heard to say, in not a very quiet voice, to the girl who was taking out one of their rides "Take care of the horses, but it doesn't matter if you come home without the Krauts". Political correctness was not in his make up. It was one of his more favourite sayings that "if you've got a breastplate, you don't need a girth!" by which he meant that if your balance was any good the minimal help that a breastplate gives to keep the saddle in the right place should be adequate.

Rosemary was – perhaps I should say is as she is still alive and kicking strongly today - less abrasive but even she did not suffer fools gladly and it has always seemed a miracle to me that the business not only survived until David died, but is still going strong today.

So, because I knew it a little, the decision to go to Devon was not a difficult one to make. When my mother heard about it, she commented "But, darling, does anyone really live in Devon?" She meant, of course, anyone with whom we would want to make friends and, long before she died in 1989, she had her answer. We have so many good and close friends from all walks of life in the West Country that, when we meet someone new, I always curse under my breath and wonder how we will cope with entertaining and being entertained by yet more people.

In our early days down here, however, there were two things that gave us a particularly easy entree into Devon society. The first was the birth of my daughter six months after we moved, and the second was our interest in horses and hunting. As I have already said, I originally gave up riding when I was nine, in order to do more fishing during our infrequent family holidays in the country, but after my divorce I slowly started to ride again. By the time I re-married I had bought a huge cart mare in partnership with a couple I met at some stables under the Sussex Downs. A few lessons and a good deal of self teaching somehow resulted in my becoming a relatively safe rider, doing little harm to myself or, more importantly, the horse and by the time we moved west I was ready, if somewhat uneasy about it, to try a days hunting.

Although we took Betsy to Devon with us, her co-owners having lost interest in her, it was clear that she was quite unsuitable as a hunter. We put her in foal with the idea of breeding a heavy weight hunter of which there was a huge shortage at that time. The result was Snooker, who was somewhat lighter than we had planned but still a success. He came in the first five a number of times in hunter youngstock classes at various shows, and finally won one of these as a two year old at a small show at Lympstone. We should have kept him and, had we done so, he would have made a wonderful horse for me in five years or so: but we sold him. It was a big mistake. He was said to have developed "curby hocks", which knocked his value down to £1100, for which we disposed of him to a girl not far away, who planned to "bring him on"! She did so so successfully that she sold him as a four year old for £3500 and he duly became a grade A show jumper, well known on the circuit, especially in Essex. It is always somebody else who makes money out of horses.

We sold Betsy as well and she was said to have been seen out hunting with the South Devon although I never really believed this.

Meanwhile we made the first of our two really good buys in the horse world. From Exmoor came a 15.2 hh grey gelding aged 7 called Toby. Jenny, and, on occasions, I hunted him for seventeen years: he never went wrong, he was good tempered and charming in every way and very greatly loved. He went well round a hunter trial course and across the moor. Lest he should sound a bit boring, I should add that he did have two faults. He was positively dangerous in traffic: you never knew when he was going to take exception to a lorry or a signpost which made the whole business of exercising him a somewhat nerve wracking experience, and we kept him off main roads as much as possible. He was also very unreliable when being loaded into a trailer. When we went to collect him from North Devon, in a borrowed trailer, we had a puncture on the way home. After unloading him to get the tyre mended - there was no spare which was quite normal in Devon - we could not get him back in again. Having tried all the approved tricks and quite a few best left unmentioned, we arranged with a local farmer to keep him for the night, planning to collect him next day in a lorry. Arriving at the farm, to which we walked him up the main A38 with some trepidation, the farmer suggested that we park the trailer in a gateway and try again. He walked straight in.

Some time later Jenny ended a rare and long days hunting on Exmoor as darkness fell. Having ridden back to the trailer Toby refused point blank to load. Ronnie Wallace and Jimmy Hill appeared on the scene but their combined efforts and experience was no match for Toby. Jenny ended up hacking him back through the moonlight to where she was staying for the night.

Despite the fact that he never lost these two disadvantages, Toby remained a firm favourite.

The problem of finding a horse for Jenny having been solved, we turned our attentions to finding a mount for me. This was more difficult. There was no way I could be regarded as anything other than a beginner and our first buy was a disaster. We found a TB mare called Meavy. She was a beautiful ride and, once on her back, she was everything one could have asked for. I had my first ever days hunting on her with the Eggesford and could turn her on a sixpence, with one hand, in a rubber snaffle. Unfortunately she had a screw loose. She was impossible to catch - she had to be corralled first, be groomed and then saddled, before you went to her head. This was not ideal. She also would not load - not just now and again but, with the exception of when we brought her home from near the Cornish border, never. It was quickly clear that this would not work and we sold her on to a farmer at Ashreigney about twenty miles away. He arrived with a trailer to collect her assuring us that he would get her into it without trouble. An hour later he started the long hack home.

Meavy had a foal the following year, trod on it and broke its leg. She was that sort of mare.

Our next effort was a good deal better. We found a 15 hh coloured mare, again up in the Exmoor area. She was beautifully bred by the well known stallion Pony Express and could look a picture. She was easily managed, loaded well, gave me some fabulous days hunting on the moor and although, after we had had her for about a year, she could get a little nasty in her box, we would have kept her had she not developed a problem with her wind. This resulted from an unusual allergy to shavings but we never cured it even when we put her back on to straw. We were forced to sell her on to someone who wanted a horse just for light hacking. She was really too small for me to be ideal.

Thus we were on the hunt yet again. Our great friends Christopher and Mary-Ann Gill - Chris was Master of the Eggesford at the time - told us about a horse called Tug, whom they said was exactly what we wanted and "a perfect gent". He was owned by Tony Carden and his wife and was said to have "a slight whistle" but in every other way to be perfectly sound. I ran into Tony, whom I already knew, at the Devon County Show in May and asked him how much he wanted for him. His reply was "£1500" which effectively killed things there and then. We did not pay that sort of money for our horses in those days. Two months later, however, we heard that he was still for sale and it was suggested to us that if we offered £900 for him it would be accepted. It was by now late July and we were in the middle of a heat wave. I rang Tony and told him that if we could agree a price of £900 in advance, we would drive to East Devon to see the horse and if we liked him we would buy him at that price. I said it would not be worth us coming forty miles and back in the heat just to discover that the price was wrong, even if the horse was right. Tony agreed and we bought this extraordinary animal home. He was 16.1 hh, dark bay and a cross between a shire and an arab. Some years later I wrote the following article about him for a magazine called South-West Horse which is now defunct. It sums up the horse and my feelings about him so well that I reproduce it here virtually in full without apology.

TWENTY FIVE YEARS ON

On a fine spring day in 1972 a bright chestnut arab mare, heavily in season, escaped from her paddock in North Devon, and set off to find a mate. The first stallion she came across was a large black shire who was only too pleased to find something rather finer and more lissom on offer than his usual heavy weight mares.

Eleven months later a strange looking foal emerged, not without difficulty and help, from the fifteen hand mare. The colt was large and gangly with obviously oversize feet and a Roman nose with a large blaze starting at eye level and ending to one side of his nostrils. By the time he had grown into a yearling, his owners had decided that he was useless to them and he was sent to the local horse market. Having turned into a coarse thick-set youngster it was clear, from the moment he entered the ring, that the meat man would be the most likely buyer. At £105 the hammer was about to fall on another purchase for the knacker man when a lady in the crowd bid £108 and secured the horse. She named him Tug.

Broken and brought on slowly as is always so necessary with big horses, the gelding proved gentle and genuine. In due course he was sold on to Tony and Christine Carden, whose son hunted him with the East Devon and took him to the odd hunter trial. Tug turned into a hugely powerful 7 yo with the large feet and feathered heels of a shire, the head of his father and a body that would have looked well placed behind a coal dray. There was, however, about him some indefinable touch of class that nobody was able to put their finger on but which clearly bore his mother's influence.

When, two years later, the Cardens found themselves with too many horses, he moved to Okehampton, complete with a whistle in his wind, front feet that paddled outwards and hind legs that plaited as he walked, when he was bought as a hunter by Neon and Jenny Reynolds.

Fourteen years on, he was still going strong. He hunted with the Mid Devon on Dartmoor for seven seasons week in and week out, carrying his owner faithfully across rocks, bogs and peat hags with minimal assistance from the saddle and without ever putting a foot wrong. Never ideally fast enough for moorland hunting, he made up for his lack of speed by the immense stamina that stemmed from both his parents and on no occasion did he feel other than fit and strong at the end of the most strenuous of days. He unfailingly pulled Neon back to the trailer at an uncomfortable and desperately tiring jog.

In his box he was a great worrier, going round and round with concern if a strange car or figure appeared in the yard or he heard horses hacking down the lane that he could not see round the corner. He was so adept at opening his door that if it was left without a clip on it for a moment he would be out behind you before you had time to look round.

In due course, when the Reynolds's went to hunt with the Lamerton and because they had no time to keep him as well as Toby and their daughter's pony at home, Tug went to live with Clive Jenkins, who was at that time running a hireling yard in Lamerton village. He was only hunted on the moor by his owner but was hired out to all and sundry on the Lamerton's "in-country" days. He thrived on this life, being tough enough – some might have said insensitive enough – to carry many people with little riding experience and he looked after a number during their first days hunting without suffering in any way. It was during this time that he gave Neon his best ever days hunting. Meeting at Prewley at the end of March, the Lamerton went, with permission, into the Mid Devon country and, late in the day, found a fox way out into the moor behind Steeperton Tor. It ran in a large circle back to Meldon near the meet, but then, instead of going to ground as most foxes would have done, it ran out again behind Yes Tor, past where hounds had found and made another large circle before finally holing up in some clitter near Belstone. Few horses were left at the end of this run which, that evening. was reckoned to have been over fifteen miles but which inevitably stretched over the next few days. Tug, at nineteen, was one of them. He has had many good days since then but his always suspect breathing has increasingly found him out.

He is hired out no more, to the disappointment of one of Clive's clients who, having had his first ever day hunting on him, asked for another day but said that he must ride Tug again. When Clive asked him why the reply was: "Well, you don't actually have to do anything on him and if you do it doesn't make any difference". It seemed a fairly dubious compliment.

Whether Tug outlives hunting or as soon as he can no longer enjoy a good day out on the moor, he will go on to more ever lasting days with hounds in another world. He has always lived for his hunting and it would not be kind to keep him when he could no longer start shivering with excitement early on a hunting morning, or prick his ears at the sound of the horn.

*   *   *

I wrote the above in 1997 and dear old Tug went on until early 1999, when he was twenty seven years old. The previous autumn Toby had gone, finally the victim of age after hunting for seven seasons on bute because of a problem with his front feet. I brought Tug back from a day on the moor dreadfully lame and it was soon clear that a tendon had gone. Bill Henderson told me that if I turned him away until May –

it was then February – he might come right for another season.

I thought it over for 24 hours and then rang Tony Boon, our huntsman. I knew it could not be right to keep him at that age and with his breathing difficulties on the off chance that he might struggle on. When Tony came I wept buckets, just as Jenny had done when Toby went.

*   *   *

It will have been noticed that, while we first went out in Devon with the Eggesford, we soon started to do most of our hunting with the Mid Devon, although in fact we continued to have the odd day with the former right up until we moved from our first Devon house at Folly Gate in 1996. Thereafter we were no longer in their country. While we subscribed to both packs it was an ideal arrangement as the Eggesford hunted solely "in-country" which means off Dartmoor, while the Mid Devon were always on the moor on Saturdays. I quickly became a devoted moorland hunter, finding the wide open spaces, the almost continuous movement and the exciting runs across every conceivable type of obstacle except jumps, exhilarating in the extreme. By contrast the lanes, gates and constant standing around "in-country" seemed tame and restricting. Sadly our relationship with the Mid Devon soured as the result of one of those appalling hunt rows that seem to dog almost every pack from time to time.

In this case few people emerged from the disaster with any great credit and certainly the reputation of hunting as a whole and the Master of Foxhounds Association in particular was left badly tarnished. Cutting a long story as short as possible, the problem was initiated by the then Master deciding to take on a most unsavoury character as his joint master for the following season. Some disagreement between the two of them about how much say in the running of the hunt each should have, led to the new joint master elect riding up to the existing Master's wife in the middle of the moor and setting about her with his hunting whip. She was taken to hospital with shock, the affair hit the headlines of the gutter press and there, we all assumed the matter would end. There seemed no possibility that such a man could be considered a fit person to become a MFH. Wishing, however, to make certain that such a disreputable character would also be unwelcome out hunting with the pack, I, together with a very few others wrote to the Chairman asking for his confirmation, not only that there could be no question of him becoming a joint master but also that he had been told that he could not hunt with the Mid Devon in future.

To our absolute dismay no such undertaking was forthcoming and the whole matter was referred to the MFHA, who backed the committee and Chairman. It was an extraordinary decision that in effect condoned a man hitting a lady. The driving force was money, the root of so much evil in the horse world as elsewhere.

In due course an Extraordinary General Meeting was called at which the sole issue was whether a completely new man and this vagabond should be appointed joint masters for the following season. There was a feeling of real devilry in the hall in Chagford that night, the voting was close, but cheque book politics won the day, behavioural considerations went out of the window and we and a number of others departed, sadder and disbelieving, to hunt elsewhere.

The Mid-Devon was, at its best, a wonderful pack. Had one written a novel based on it and the personalities in it in the eighties, it would not have been believed. Picking one story from my memory at random, there was, amongst its subscribers, a strange but highly intelligent man, who had a tendency to violence. He took up with a lady from Okehampton with whom he barricaded himself in his house. Taking fright, she managed to call the police. When the local bobby arrived he was faced with a bolted door on the inside of which was a man armed with an axe. The policeman duly received a commendation for bravery.

The same unstable character was, shortly after this episode, out hunting in the late spring after an exceptionally dry spell of weather. After lighting his pipe, he threw the match on the ground and was, in an instant, surrounded by a ring of fire."Bloody hell" somebody exclaimed, "now we've got an arsonist out with us as well as a mad axeman!"

The chap in question was indeed a most odd man. He was highly educated: in conjunction with somebody else he wrote a book about equestrian equipment that was very well thought of in the horse world, although he knew nothing about horses at all. Just before he left Devon and was, as far as I know, never seen again, he suddenly announced that he was really some foreign Duke and the next telephone book duly printed his number under the name of the Duke of somewhere or other in, I believe, Portugal. His strangeness just about summed up all that was most entertaining and at the same time most irritating about the hunt in the '80's.

Having decided that we had to leave the Mid-Devon, the obvious way to go was west, to the Lamerton and the Spooner's and West Dartmoor and with both these packs we met new friends and had a great deal of fun. Again we restricted ourselves mainly to moorland hunting until Jenny had a nasty fright one day and, not helped by the fact that we had just lost the roof to our house, literally, in a major gale, somewhat lost her nerve. Thereafter for a few seasons I hunted on Dartmoor and she went in-country. Gradually things returned to normal and when in time we moved a few miles west to Bridestowe we were deep in the Lamerton country and became more and more involved with that pack.

After the old, much loved geriatrics went, we looked for a horse to share between us and lit upon a very common Irish hunter type who had just come over from Ireland. Beamish, as we called him, was almost a clone of Tug. He was pretty poor when he arrived with us but made up quickly into a solid and rather bulky 15.3 hh gelding. On getting him home we got our most excellent vet. Bill Henderson to come and look at him. Apart from pronouncing him to have too much liquid in his lungs, which was easily remediable, he passed him fit and asked how old he was meant to be. He had been sold to us as a ten year old with good hunting experience. Bill took a quick look at his teeth and said "Well, he might be seven but I would put him at six!" Whilst in a way this meant that we had bought a bargain, it also gave rise to a few problems. He was far greener than we had wanted and whilst there was not an ounce of malice in him, he did have a few dislikes that caused us a little initial difficulty. He would not walk across a wet patch in road, let alone through a puddle and this lead us to believe that he had been badly bogged in Ireland. By gently working on this. we got him more reasonable about water but jumping a stream is still not easy and he has a habit of stopping at anything that involves even slightly soft ground. This is the reverse of ideal on the moor and, as anything like a ditch or large rock that was somewhat unexpected also resulted in the brakes being applied extremely hard, my first efforts at hunting him did lead to a few falls, all of them thankfully with a soft landing.

He once stopped dead and catapulted me over his head when I was riding out on the moor with a lady friend – or perhaps I should say a friend who was a lady. We were on the edge of one of the Dartmoor firing areas and firing was in progress. Beamish took off into the danger area but out of a small barn near its boundary came a ranger carrying a yellow bucket. As Beamish has his feed out of exactly that he walked quietly up to the man and started eating. He was re-delivered to me with solicitous enquiries as to whether I was O.K., which I was, and we continued our ride undamaged. We have now reached a degree of mutual respect and understanding for each other, have had some lovely days together and I would hate to get rid of him. It is nevertheless a fact that he is not totally ideal. He is a big and somewhat unmanageable horse for Jenny, he is too slow to be really good on the moor and, being an excellent doer, he is extremely hard work to get fit. But he is kind, gentle and a real character. As we get older we no longer need to try to prove to ourselves or anyone else that we can stay out a moment longer than we actually want to, and galloping downhill across Dartmoor's uncertain going is no longer essential. Beamish will stay with us just as long as we continue to want to keep a horse and I sincerely hope that a ban on hunting will not hasten a decision to give up riding sooner than we otherwise would.

* * *

For those who have never done any moorland hunting I should try to explain in a few lines what it entails.

The first thing to say is that there is nothing poncy or stuck up about hunting in the West Country. I have heard of packs "up-country" where mackintoshes are frowned on and even one where to turn up the collar of one's coat is regarded as unacceptable. What a lot of rubbish that is. Down here there are all too often days when a good riding mac is essential: more frowned on are red coats worn by members of the field and top hats are almost, but not quite, laughed at.

At one point the infamous James Hewitt came to live near us at Bratton Clovelly. We had known him for some time as he used to come into our shop, The Exeter Saddlers, which we bought when we moved west. Whilst perhaps spoilt, I had always found him both charming and polite as a customer and was as outraged as were so many others when he behaved as he did after his affair with Princess Diana. However, what irritated me most was when he turned up for a Wednesday's hunting with the Lamerton dressed in a swallowtail coat and top hat. He looked, and I hope felt, a fool.

Just as I should be terrified if I went up to the Shires and found myself faced by enormous fences of some sort, were they walls, tiger traps or hedges, so people from up-country arrive for a days hunting on Dartmoor only to find themselves amazed by what we accept as everyday hazards. It is perhaps the unexpected that finds out the visitors and causes so many empty saddles. Setting off sedately enough, one glances at very hilly country well strewn with rocks, the odd track and mile upon mile of open grassland that appears from a distance to be wonderful galloping country. The colours of the fairly sparse vegetation change, often every fifty yards or so, giving a clue to the experienced eye what going lies beneath it. Numerous streams criss cross the moor and these are often edged by unstable banks: knowing where the safe crossing places are is a vital part of hunting on Dartmoor. Huge areas of rocks, known as clitter, abound. Few of these are impassable at a walk but crossing a hundred yards of clitter can often leave one half a mile behind the field that has circumnavigated it. Bogs abound. Most are relatively shallow affairs, unlikely to cause serious damage to either horse or rider but extremely unseating. Now and again one encounters a deeper one that can be dangerous. I remember a day out with the Spooners when half the field got themselves into a bog where the horses were plunging tummy deep into it every five or six strides. With everyone dismounted, nobody was certain of the way out on to firm ground. Nerves were somewhat shattered by the time we extricated ourselves and the whipper-in, riding up alongside my wife a moment later commented: "Uncertain going, madam!".

With a fox found and running out across the moor, hounds on and all set fair for a good run, the field spreads out on a broad front, one eye on the line the fox is taking, the other on the ground. A good moorland horse will pick his way amongst the obstacles with total ease, adjusting his stride as necessity demands, but no horse will keep up if he is piloted straight into the rocks or bogs or has to waste time finding a place to cross a stream because his rider thinks he knows what he is doing, only to find that more experieneced people are taking a longer but faster route. Often reaching the top of a hill, hounds can be spotted a mile away, still running hard. Will they turn left or right when they reach that bog? If they go left, so one's mind runs, I can hack along the top of this ridge, drop down off it before the next Tor, and meet up with them again. If they go right I must go back down the hill I have just toiled up and cross the stream by the only crossing place within a mile to, hopefully, come up with them again by the marshy ground at the source. A moment of indecision is actually helpful, giving time for hounds, casting around in the distance, to settle on a line to the left. Gently one sets off along the ridge. The problem now is to avoid heading Charlie. Keeping high one gets a wonderful view of hounds hunting along below one as they get nearer and nearer. Eventually they pass and one can canter slowly down the hill to fit in behind the Huntsman and the only one of the Masters still up with hounds. Behind one the field, on tiring horses, is amazed to see us again, believing us left well behind. A sense of conceited satisfaction is unavoidable. However, the alternative is less attractive. Having moved too fast and turned the wrong way, one finds oneself alone at the top of the stream, nobody in sight, no sound except the wind. The only thing to do is to turn for home, keeping an eye open all the way: stopping and listening at intervals. Luck may put one in touch again, more likely a good day has been ruined by getting too far behind early in the run. Field sports again!

*   *   *

Of course there are other things to riding apart from hunting.

I love simply to hack across the moor at any time of year, alone or in company, probably from one pub to another, learning slowly about the archaeology of Dartmoor and its fascinating history. Getting the horse fit is less entertaining. Hours round the lanes are boring for me and uninteresting for the horse but has to be done.

Jenny used to take Toby to the odd hunter trial. Totally unconcerned about winning, jumping round the course was fun in itself for both of them. We got involved inevitably with the Pony Club when our daughter was young and went to shows and gymkhanas seemingly ad infinitum until, like most children she grew out of ponies almost overnight. I did the announcing at one of the local point-to-points for a few years – not to be confused with commentating. Having loved going racing in years gone by, I had a lot of the patter somehow tucked away in my mind and rather enjoyed this job.

The whole equestrian scene gave us many good friends and acquaintances, provided an entrée into local society, that we might well have struggled to achieve unless we had been horse orientated, and has given us tremendous fun, albeit at very considerable cost. Not least our ability to ride reasonably well led to two memorable holidays. We happened to wander on to the African Horse Safari stand at Badminton one year and slowly a plan evolved in our minds to go and ride with the animals rather than to goggle at them. After a lot of planning we set off for Botswana in 1997 to ride in the Okavango Delta with Barney and P-J Bestelink of Okavango Horse Safaris. Wanting to be out of this country during the winter, we made our trip in February and despite having the most wonderful time, realised that, with no water in the delta at that time of year, we had probably not gone at the most interesting time of the year. On our return I wrote an article, which was duly printed in the then well thought of but now deceased magazine, "Riding", with which Barney was so pleased that she offered us another holiday at half price. This was an offer that could clearly not be refused (although I felt some embarrassment as I knew she had not gained much business as a result of it) and we organised our second venture into the Okavango in August 1999 arranging to follow our safari with ten days in Zimbabwe.

When we got out to Botswana, the really good rains experienced in the Angolan Highlands in April had spread down through the whole of the Okavango and our magic experiences of the previous year were quickly surpassed.

Transferring from Air Botswana – reputed to be the most expensive airline in the world mile for mile - at Maun into a light aircraft, we could see the floods in the Delta almost as soon as we took off for the airstrip at Xudum and as soon as we arrived there after the 40 minute flight it was clear that the water was extremely high. We had not, however, bargained for this to be impressed on us quite so soon or quite so forcibly as it was when the Toyota 4x4 pick up sent to transfer us to base camp became irrevocably stuck, axle deep, halfway through the hours journey. Endless jacking up and placing logs under the wheels proved fruitless and one of our fellow guests, an attractive young physiotherapist from Bristol began to look increasingly incongruous in a mini dress and sandals while, as darkness fell and the inevitable light hearted talk of lions and buffalo began to seem slightly less amusing, the other guest with us, a German divorcee, found her sense of humour less and less equal to the situation!

The nights are cool in Botswana in August and we were all grateful when the lights of a rescuing Landrover could be seen approaching through the bush. A cheery greeting from PJ boosted our morale and we were soon pulled out and on our way again. After a couple of welcoming whiskies, a good dinner, and a few moments chat round the camp fire, we collapsed thankfully into bed in our comfortable tent to make up for a rather sleepless night on the 747 from London to Jo'burg.

Six o'clock next morning seemed to come all too soon, but we were somehow all mounted by the time the light strengthened at seven, and the four of us staying for five nights rather than ten, set off with Barney across the bush to a secondary camp for two nights. One's fellow riders are all important on such a holiday and I was sorry that we had the German lady for company instead of the blonde physio (Jenny disagreed!), but in fact the former turned out to be a splendid and educated companion. The other member of our group was an American called, inevitably, Chuck, who was the best sort of Yank, being well travelled, well educated and very knowledgeable.

I rode a 17 hh TB and my wife was on another slightly smaller one, both being very forward going but entirely manageable. We quickly experienced the pleasure of wading the horses through the warm water, often up to their tummies, and once had to stop and hitch cameras and binoculars up to shoulder level, while the groom carrying the loaded rifle had to remove it from its holster and carry it above his head when we rode across a deep river that forced the horses to swim for a few strides leaving us wet to the tops of our thighs. The quickly warming sun dried us off in a few minutes while all the time we were sighting a seemingly endless quantity of game, often at very close range, including particularly giraffe and many different varieties of antelope.

After a stop for chocolate and oranges, the plan was to picket the horses for lunch about twelve, have a siesta in the bush and then push on to camp about three pm. Suddenly a whistle from the groom riding at the rear of the six strong party, warned us of something more exciting and we became aware of five pairs of ears peeping over the top of the bush about 100 yards away. Most people on safari long to see lions but if you are on horseback it is not good news. Lions love horsemeat and avoiding action is always essential as quickly as possible. "I think we'll do a bit of island hopping and try and leave them undisturbed" said Barney and, keeping a close look out behind us, we waded through the reeds until we were at a safer distance from which we could watch through binoculars the pride, in their turn, still watching us.

The back-up team had lunch ready for us when we rendez-vous'd with them and after a siesta (following which Barney displayed a considerable degree of sadism when spraying some appallingly stingy antiseptic on my foot which had become infected after I had stepped on sharp log while trying to unbog the vehicle the previous evening), we had another lovely ride during which we saw both elephant and giraffe wading slowly through the floods, the former spraying themselves with water just like Ba-Ba. We eventually arrived at a new and beautiful camp set amidst the water, where a hippo was grazing not far away. Our tent had a well worn path running up beside it but it was not a path made by man! Throughout the night we could hear large animals sploshing through the water but none came too close. Next morning another ride took us to a fantastically lovely lagoon where up to a dozen hippos were alternately lying quietly with just their ears and nostrils out of the water, and cavorting aggressively around in the deeps. Barney told us to be ready to canter off quickly if any of them showed signs of making for the bank! Apparently they do this underwater and you only know they are coming when you see a large bow wave! Rather sadly, I thought, they stayed in the water. Shortly afterwards we were lucky enough to get a lengthy and beautiful view of the very rare Pel's fishing owl. This huge bird, pale gold in colour, and about 30 ins long, sat obligingly in a tree, looking down on us in a rather superior way before taking off, almost, it seemed, in slow motion and giving us a wonderful view of his 8 ft wingspan.

During our siesta disaster struck! The horses, which always graze loose but carefully watched, had been spooked by something and had all taken off into the bush. Barney had rushed after them in the LR but after two hours there had been no sightings of them and concern was growing. On a previous occasion when something similar had happened, one horse had indeed been taken by a lion and another, badly mauled, had had to be put down shortly afterwards.

To take our minds off things, we were taken for a mokoru (canoe) trip in the evening to see crocodiles and birds and had the added bonus of sitting quietly just underneath a tree on which a large fish eagle was unconcernedly searching the lagoon for his supper.

Not until we got back to camp were we told that the previous guests had been chased by a hippo at the end of their mokoru trip and that hippos often come up under canoes and just "chomp" them in half - plus their cargo!

Just as we settled down to supper, news came through on the radio that seven of the eight horses had wandered into base camp 15 miles away, just before sunset. Wonderful as this was, we all remained greatly concerned about Matabele, Barney's lead horse, who had only just joined the outfit and was therefore far less experienced in the ways of the bush than the rest.

With nothing to ride, we set off early next morning in the LR to return to base camp by a roundabout route, that would take us past two or three places were Matabele had been reported being seen, but there was no sign of him. We did come across a pride of lions and took the opportunity of being in a vehicle rather than on horseback, to stop and watched as they lay lazily under a tree. They hardly looked at us, having eyes only for a number of vultures that were circling in the sky behind us, obviously waiting for the right moment to descend on a kill when its owner left it.

We drove into base camp about noon. We didn't need to ask Barney what news there was of Matabele. Her face, wreathed in smiles and at the same time with tears running down her cheeks, said it all. He had staggered into camp at dawn, tired and traumatised, but otherwise unhurt.

With our original horses clearly due for "r and r" and with PJ with the other half of the guests just having moved out to the camp that we had just left, there were relatively few for Barney to choose from for our evening ride. I found myself on Malomb, who had been rescued not all that long before, from pulling a coal cart in Soweto! It was quickly clear that he had fully recovered from his past experiences as he immediately took a strong hold. I had to be very careful not to let him get away from me as I was seriously concerned that I might never get him back! I had visions of the two of us disappearing into the bush for ever! He was a tremendous character and although I would not have enjoyed coping with him on a long ride, those two hours were highly entertaining if somewhat testing.

Jenny rode a beautiful young TB with a suspect leg who thankfully seemed to get sounder as time went on. There is not a bad horse on the strength.

The plan for the next morning was to have a quiet ride from seven until about ten, stop for a brunch cooked over an open fire in the bush, and ride back to base again. The best laid plans can quickly be upset on safari and we were about to be treated to a prime example of this. We sighted a leopard for the first time in our three visits to Africa but on arriving at the pre-arranged spot for brunch, where Person, the Bestelink's right hand man, had everything laid out to perfection with eggs, bacon, sausages, mushrooms and liver were being fried over an open fire, we were met with the news that a pride of eleven lions were resting 500 yards away. A decision had to be quickly taken as to whether we could stay and eat or must move on out of danger. No sooner had Barney decided to stay than all the horses started neighing and Person was despatched to find out whether the lions had been alerted to the possibility of an easy lunch. He returned with the bad news that the male had stalked off to our left where the picnic spot was unprotected by water, while the lionesses had circled off to the right! There was no alternative but to gulp down the delicious meal, mount and move on.

Riding back to camp Barney made the remark that was to become a classic for us. Approaching a wide bit of water about 3 ft deep, she made hushing signs and whispered rather loudly, "We must go quickly and quietly through here. It can be a bit croc-y"!

We were all amused rather than frightened by this because, as the German said, "Barney might take a risk with her guests, but she certainly wouldn't with her horses!" From the word go Barney makes it clear, with, of course, immense charm, that the welfare of her guests comes a poor second to that of her horses.

Approaching camp for the final time we removed our saddles and bridles, leaving them to be collected by mokoru with our binoculars and cameras, and swam the horses bareback across a deep part of the river. I fell off, lay on my back in the warm water and slowly kicked my way to the bank. It seemed a magical way to end a marvellous few days.

Luckily it wasn't a croc-y place!

* * *

After leaving the delta we flew up to Victoria Falls - well worth a short visit despite the "trippery" atmosphere - and then on to Harare, where we hired a car and drove around the eastern part of Zimbabwe. We had one wonderful ride across the hills above Chimanimani, looking down eastwards towards the Mozambique border. How sad that, within six months of our visit, such a wonderful country was being raped by so much greed, evil and corruption.

* * *

Some years ago the then Hon. Sec. of the Lamerton Foxhounds, Elizabeth Bury and her husband Michael, hit on the idea of organising a post hunting season ride across Dartmoor, staying the night at a pub in the middle of the moor and riding back next day.

Over the years this has developed into the annual "Hexworthy" ride when a number of close friends, all intrepid Dartmoor hunters and all with the same attitude to life, are invited by the organisers to ride with them to the Forest Inn at Hexworthy. It is vital that everyone involved has a roughly similar sense of humour - not too lewd but certainly not too strait laced! Non riding husbands or wives are welcomed for dinner and then to stay the night, which helps to avoid the dangers of having to decide which unaccompanied ladies can share a room - that is with other ladies, you understand! The

166

pub can accommodate a maximum of about 16 people, so that the ride is never in danger of becoming too large and the landlord, Alan Selwood, lays on a superb dinner in a private room - a necessity in view of the hilarity which follows a day in the fresh air, interspersed and followed by a reasonable, but of course never excessive, amount of alcohol.

Previous rides have involved a few disasters when people, "certain of the route", have suddenly found that a bridge marked on the map is only a footbridge or that a place, previously easily traversed, has turned into a deep bog. Once the ride was so badly delayed that the riders arrived at the pub in a thoroughly bad temper only shortly before dinner time. On another occasion a valuable point-to-pointer, due to run eight days later, suddenly found itself first negotiating some potentially leg breaking clitter and then plunged stifle deep in a bog. It still ran very well!

These events have, however, impressed on those involved, none of whom should have needed this added warning, that Dartmoor is not to be trifled with and the route is nowadays always carefully reconnoitred in advance.

This year, for the third time, the ride was organised and the recce-ing carried out by the author and the second loveliest lady in the Lamerton (the loveliest being, of course, my wife!). Four days of riding on the moor in the spring in such company is, naturally, a major pleasure and we both thoroughly enjoy this essential prerequisite to the ride itself. With the occasional help of well known local Dartmoor artist, John Christian, we not only saw parts of Dartmoor new to us, but learnt a good deal about its history and archaeology. We traversed leats built by POW's during the Napoleonic wars, found new crossing places over streams, doused for energy and water lines by stone circles and looked at 15 ft high menhirs at the end of stone rows. From afar we looked down on the infamous Foxtor Mire, the largest and most dangerous bog on the moor, and lunched next to the Crazy Well Pool. This was said to be bottomless after it had, according to legend, been sounded by tying all the bell ropes from the local church together without them touching the bottom. Sad to say some more modern spoilsport came along and found it to be no more than 15 ft deep!

We plunged through an increasingly deep and unstable approach to one stream crossing, actually marked as a bridleway by the National Parks Authority, only to end up both sitting on the damp ground with our horses up to the roots of their tails in a bog! Shortly afterwards we became involuntarily separated when one of us pushed on through some appalling clitter and the other decided that the holes between each rock were actually inviting the horses to break their legs and, rather more sensibly, turned back. Neither of these routes seemed ideal places through which to take a dozen other riders!

Having decided that this year, in view of advancing years, the ride should be rather shorter than in the past, we chose the route, recce-ed every yard of it, invited the right number of guests for the right number of rooms, and sat back to wait for the usual flood of late disasters to destroy all our plans. This year it was a more than usually large number of unfit or lame horses that nearly upset the applecart. However, by dint of relying on the kindness of friends, and making the right soothing noises to those that had not been asked on the ride but who owned an ideal horse for it, everyone ended up on something with four sound legs although more than one mount quickly proved to have no mouth at all! A late cri de coeur from someone who demanded an en-suite room because they had to get up at least twice in the night, having been turned down, all that was now needed was a fine weekend.

Arriving at the farm at Sampford Spiney, where one of the Lamerton's joint masters had kindly agreed to let us leave our trailers and lorries (on a previous ride one person had returned on the Sunday to find his trailer missing two wheels!), there were vehicles parked higgledy-piggledy in such a way that, whilst there was masses of room for everyone, late arrivals found their way blocked by at least two Discoveries left in eccentric places. Having finally caught the attention of their owners, persuaded them to stop chattering for a moment and move them, the conversation turned to the weather forecast. Half the riders knew for a fact that it was going to be a fine, sunny day, getting quite warm, while the remainder were equally convinced that the mist would be down before we got to the pub.

It was little consolation to those of the former persuasion that it turned out to be a lovely evening by the time we arrived, because earlier we had to endure 90 minutes of very wet Dartmoor rain, driven by an increasingly strong westerly wind. Only one person had put on a long mac, whilst one neither wore nor took with her anything waterproof at all! It was therefore perhaps fortuitous that after 100 minutes riding with everyone getting colder by the minute, we had planned to meet up with another of the joint masters' wives, who plied us with either white wine or port. The port went very quickly! With the mist coming down, the unwaterproofed lady showing distinct signs of hypothermia, with everyone's nether regions getting increasingly damp and bad temper threatening to break out, we stopped for lunch in the deep declivity of some old mine workings. We were meant to be sitting beside Crazy Well Pool in the sunshine!

Luckily this proved to be the low spot of the weekend. As we moved off again the mist cleared, the opposite hillside reappeared and the sun came out. We reached the spot where we could look down on Plymouth Sound glinting ten miles away and passed Eylesbrook Tin mine, where I dismounted to look over the edge of a seemingly bottomless mine shaft. To cries of "be careful" as I slipped down to the edge of the hole over the wet grass, I found, to my chagrin, that it was only about 10 ft deep! However, I peered apparently carefully over the lip, telling everyone that I could not even see the bottom.

We rode on past Nun's Cross, dating back to 1200 ad and its farm, enclosed about 1800 but now abandoned. We searched the hillside for a sign of Childe's Tomb, where the famous hunter got caught in a blizzard: despite killing and disembowelling his horse and climbing inside it to escape the worst of the elements, he died. Waste of a horse.

On past the devilishly isolated but still inhabited cottages at Whiteworks mine, we cantered over the open ground to the ford over the Swincombe Brook and so to the Forest Inn.

It was warm enough to sit outside the hotel to drink our tea after turning the horses out all together in the field - it pays not to look too carefully at the fencing! - but hot baths soon called and for most of us a snatch of sleep followed. The bar, however, seemed irresistible by 7.30 where, to my total amazement, everyone decided virtually at once and with no more than about two changes of mind what they wanted to eat.

As can be imagined dinner for sixteen took a little time to prepare, but this 45 minute delay gave an ideal amount of time for adequate consumption of gins and tonics to give dinner a good start. The splendid meal that followed was helped down by ten bottles of wine that settled nicely on top of the g & t's. The noise level got out of hand pretty quickly but only really became noticeable when one left the table to visit the loo. We clearly did not drink too much as everyone put away a "full house" breakfast at 8.45 next morning without reproducing it. Quite a feat!

In that it was raining before we set off for home, the weather was better on Sunday, allowing everyone to reach for their long riding macs in the certainty that they would need them. We negotiated the high moor in safety, failed to fall into the leat alongside which we rode for half an hour, successfully found the aqueduct and waterfall on it dating back 1794 and still as good today as they were over 200 years ago, groped through the mist to a well recognisable path and dismounted safely but tiredly at Sampford Spiney as forecast on the dot of 2pm.

A weekend's riding in wonderful company, amidst glorious scenery (when we could see it!) with almost endless laughs, I recommend something similar to everyone who is lucky enough to live near the right sort country.

*   *   *

As I write this in the summer of 2002, the future of hunting remains as uncertain as ever.[1] So many words have been written about it that I will restrict myself to very few. While disagreeing profoundly with them, I nevertheless respect the views of those who genuinely disapprove of hunting for animal welfare reasons. Amongst the anti-hunting brigade such people are few and those that exist neither listen to the arguments nor have any knowledge of what they are trying to abolish.

The really appalling opponents of hunting are those who, in addition to those same shortcomings, hold no thoughts for the welfare of the fox, disregard totally the effect that a ban would have on hounds, horses and jobs, and are simply interested in doing away with something that they believe is a rich man's sport that is enjoyed only by the privileged, whom they abhor.

Brought down to basics and talking about fox-hunting alone, the position is simple:

The fox has no predators apart from man

The fox has to be controlled

Only man can do this

He has four methods that he can employ – hunting, shooting, gassing, snaring

Of these hunting is, at worst arguably, and at best definitely, the most humane.

It therefore follows that where it is possible to control foxes by hunting rather than by any other method, hunting should continue.

Commonsense tells one that this argument must and will prevail, but such is the lack of this most important commodity in our society today, that one has to fear that the obvious decision will be rejected in favour of one born of ill informed political dogma, ignorance and prejudice.

At the risk of repeating an awful cliche,[2] I so dread a day coming when the horn will no longer be heard, when the music of hounds will have gone for ever and the picture in

[1] By the end of the year things looked more optimistic again.
[2] Cliches may be appalling but they are often so truthful!

171

one's mind of the huntsman working his hounds along the steep side of a Dartmoor hill or a river bank will be just a memory.

CHAPTER ELEVEN

NEW ZEALAND

When my mother died and left me a little money, we went to Kenya. Later, when my father-in-law died we went and rode in Botswana and when my mother-in-law followed him we fulfilled, at least for me, a lifetime's ambition and took off for five weeks to New Zealand. Being something of a traditionalist – my wife always says my views are somewhere to the right of Attila the Hun's – and strongly anglophile, I have always wanted to visit a country where the best of these two characteristics are, I have been told, combined with a realistic attitude to the present, resulting in two lovely islands being relatively unspoilt and yet fully up-to-date.

New Zealand has a total population of just three million, of whom almost two thirds live within easy reach of Auckland, while a high proportion of the remainder are equally near Wellington; this inevitably leaves huge parts of the North Island and most of the more beautiful South Island almost uninhabited. A short geography lesson would be neither totally out of place nor uninteresting but this book is about fishing and naturally it was for the fishing that I, and, to a lesser extent my wife, wanted to visit the only part of the world outside Britain where I could happily live.

The first thing for a rather independent minded salmon fisherman to do when planning a trip to New Zealand, is to forget all about salmon. The second is to accept that without a guide your efforts at catching trout will be virtually useless. You must re-organise your very set mind completely before you leave home, make certain you have booked a really good guide with a sense of humour and great patience and realise that the trout of New Zealand will give you as great a challenge as any salmon. In fact they will provide you with a far greater opportunity to show your skill, or be constantly embarrassed by your lack of it, than will any salmon.

All the fishing is on a catch and release basis. Being a strong opponent of this in the U.K., I thought it might worry me in New Zealand, but, in truth, I never felt either any qualms or any regrets about it. Both wild brownies and rainbows run into double figures on a reasonably frequent basis but, depending on where one is fishing, 4 or 5 lbs might be regarded as the norm. They are strong fish and fast as lightning.

The streams and rivers vary greatly. One day one might be fishing on a gin clear river about the size and strength of the Lower Oykel, with a depth varying from a couple of feet to ten. The next one might be on something never more than six feet wide or three feet deep, of almost uniform depth and fast flowing throughout. Yet again, on the third day, one could be beside what looked little more than a low clear brook, in places narrowing to a tiny trickle, never appearing to be more than two feet deep. The clarity of the water leads to this constant misreading of New Zealand waters as such shallow looking places can often turn out to be five feet deep or more. In all these places giant trout will be seen rising almost imperceptibly or gently "nymphing" beneath the surface. "Seen" is, of course, to us mere mortals a misleading word to use for more often than not we will not see these fish. The guide will.

Remembering that my wife and I simply are not and never have been trout fishermen and that we were often fishing with 12 or even 18 ft leaders sometimes of only 2 lbs breaking strain and generally casting into a strong upstream wind, I regarded our results as something of a triumph. At the end of the week I asked our guide how many trout he thought a good dry fly fisherman would have brought to the net, if he had been fishing instead of us. "At least double" was his reply but I believe it might have been more than that.

Twenty-four trout to the equivalent of one rod in a week with an average weight of 4 lbs and the largest fish nearly 8 lbs. caught by anglers entirely devoid of the skills needed for the upstream dry fly and nymph fishing methods that they employed: taken from an incredible variety of different types of rivers and streams often amidst magnificent snow-capped mountain scenery, whilst seeing just two other anglers during the week. That was what we achieved in this anglers' paradise.

After the famine years on the Oykel already related and being, hopefully only temporarily, disenchanted with flogging salmon rivers in Scotland with very little reward, Jenny, and I started to look for alternative places to catch a few fish. We considered Canada, South America, The Falklands, Russia and Iceland before deciding that New Zealand not only offered wonderful fishing but was a place that we wanted to visit for so many other reasons as well.

The New Zealand method of trout fishing in running water is for the guide, who is absolutely essential and without whom little success can be expected, particularly for the newcomer to this marvellous country, to walk slowly upstream until he spots a fish, preferably one that is feeding, either on the surface or on nymphs and similar enticing tit bits below it. He then tells the fisherman exactly where the trout is, decides on what to put over it - we used Dad's Favourites, about size 16, for practically all rising fish and Pheasant Tail nymphs or Willow Bugs for the deeper feeders - and coaches his client until the fly is correctly presented and duly taken, ignored or the trout put down by the irresponsible clumsiness of the angler.

The choice of guide is, of course, all important but at the same time is a lottery. All guides who are members of their Association will undoubtedly know their stuff and be good value for money but what is so essential is also to find someone with whom it is a pleasure to spend the days and, in our case, whose patience is up to dealing with one's incompetence and the resultant disappointments.

We were incredibly lucky. We answered an advertisement in "Trout and Salmon" from Steve Gerrard, who guides out of Methven on the Canterbury Plains near Christchurch. His literature and website seemed to offer us all we could want and he booked us into an excellent farmhouse b&b nearby. Each day, Steve collected us at 7.30 am - not exactly a rest cure! He turned out to be a slim 35 year old Kiwi with a quiet unassuming manner, a lovely dry sense of humour and endless, endless patience. Brought up locally, he knew each nook and cranny of every river and stream for miles around and added to this knowledge an uncanny ability to spot fish in the most unlikely places and at a very long range.

For those with inexperienced eyes that cannot see the fish in the larger rivers, waiting for it to rise to a dry fly or for a tug on the nymph is indescribably exciting, but, in the gin clear water of the smaller streams even fairly blind old codgers like us can often see these large trout with amazing clarity: then one can watch its every move and see it turn and inspect and then either ignore or take the fly. It is at these moments that the desire to strike too soon is hard to resist!

The conversation goes something like this:

Guide: "You see that dark rock just under surface to the left of the green stone?"

Angler: "Yes".

Guide: "Well, just above it and slightly to the right of it there's a dark shadow."

Angler: "I can't see anything."

Guide: "Watch carefully 'cos it's moving about slightly the whole time – there, see it move to the right?"

Angler: "No."

Guide: "Well, it is there. Put the fly about two yards above the rock and just this side of it. Wait for it to turn after it takes the fly and then strike."

Guide: "Good – now'w'w wait, wait – strike!

Angler (transfixed): "Damn – sorry!"

Guide: "O.K. – it's not easy when you've got a nymph on. We'll try it with an indicator."

(The last word is said politely but with a certain disdain. He ties on a tiny piece of sheep's wool about three feet above the fly) "Now try again."

Angler: "Ah, I can see the fish now." He casts. "I can't see the ruddy indicator."

Guide: "Strike!!" Fish is hooked, takes off under bushes on far side of river and the leader breaks. "Bad luck. That was a really nice fish. When you hook him you must put side strain on to keep him away from those bushes."

Angler's thoughts: Hell. I didn't know I'd even hooked him before he was in the bushes – how was I meant to put side strain on him?

Guide's thoughts: Hell, I've got one here who can't see and can't play a fish either!

Of course things often go better than this thankfully, and the weeks fishing we had out of Methven in Canterbury was a wonderful experience: strange successes were mixed with considerable failures and on the best day we had six trout averaging over 6 lbs.

Certainly we missed many fish that an even half competent dry fly fisherman would have hooked. We struck too early, we struck too late, we struck too hard or not hard enough. We frequently found that we were feet short of the fish one cast and so far over it the next that it saw the line and was gone! When we did succeed in hooking a fish the chances of landing it seemed little more than evens! These big New Zealand trout know their territory all too well and move far faster than a salmon. Not only that but they make their first move towards any available cover or snags only fractions of a second after being hooked and before we, at any rate, had them "on the reel" and under any sort of control. When you add into the equation that you are playing grilse sized trout on the lightest of tackle, you can understand the relief we felt every time a fish did actually come to the net.

On the first morning Steve took us up the famous glacier fed Rakaia River, coloured a bright but pale aquamarine blue from the melting ice, to a spot where a clearer tributary entered the main river from the foothills of the mountains. A downstream wind was blowing with increasing force and handling a twelve foot leader made the task of covering a fish even a few yards upstream seem impossible. Despite the fact that it was not the trout at which she was aiming, Jenny, however, soon hooked a good fish which came off for no apparent reason. The arrangement is that one fishes in turn and watching is often as entrancing as actually casting. It was now my turn and after several attempts I finally got my fly over a fish of about 4 lbs, actually saw the rise, struck and hooked it seemingly perfectly. Any euphoria I might have felt at this early success was quickly dissipated when the hook came away and to my fury we found that it had broken at the shank! This disaster seemed doubly important when, soon afterwards, the wind now a howling gale, Steve decided we should seek more sheltered water and we retraced our way back down the Rakaia to a spring fed creek a few miles from Methven.

The comparison with where we had been earlier could not have been greater. We were now asked to fish a river varying in width from no more than a couple of feet to a maximum of about twelve, gin clear and apparently only a few inches deep. We soon learned that the depth was deceptive, the clarity of the water often leading one to assume that it was 12" deep when actually it was about 3 ft. Nevertheless in this tiny stream there was an abundance of huge trout, sometimes lying inches from the shallower bank, and all too ready to shoot off into the deeper water if they were disturbed by the slightest movement.

Here Jenny started off and at once was seconds too slow striking a large brownie that took her dry fly under the far bank. A few yards up the same pool another fish was rising quietly and for once I struck at the ideal moment, there was an explosion of spray and the fish took off down the small pool. One cannot suggest that a three pound trout will fight as long or as hard as a ten pound salmon but pound for pound they give at least as good value and we had a few alarms before Steve netted this beautiful trout and we felt that we were finally on our way.

It would be boring to list the details of each and every trout that we brought to the net during our six days with Steve. Suffice to say that after a dreadful second day when we did nothing right, I fell in and ruined the camera, and the weather turned foul after lunch necessitating an early end to a disappointingly blank day, and preceding three days of idyllic but varied success on two small streams and one larger river, during which we were introduced to "wet wading" (just shorts or trousers and trainers) and landed a total of fourteen trout averaging around 4 lbs, was sandwiched one of the most memorable days fishing of our lives.

Briefly the wind had dropped and Steve arrived at the farm trailing his jet boat. This was launched on the Rakaia, lifejackets were donned and we set off up the massive braided (many small streams between the shingle making up the whole) bright blue river. Steve wove expertly between the banks that change course after every flood and after about 20 minutes. we stepped ashore, still on the main river a few yards below a small still backwater.

Once again, as she seemed often to do in the early morning, Jenny hooked and lost a large fish within moments of starting to cast at a rise in this oasis of calm water beside the mighty Rakaia. When we had moored the boat more safely in the backwater itself, we set off upstream to where yet another tributary entered the main flow. Thus far we had only two fish to show for two days fishing and we were hardly prepared for what was to follow.

Steve spotted a large fish feeding below a rock a third of the way across a long fast pool. It appeared to me as no more than a very slightly dark shadow weaving from side to side. Steve put on a nymph with a tiny piece of sheep's wool about four foot above the fly to act as an "indicator". "If that disappears - strike!" were my instructions. Nobody was more surprised than I was when I found that I had hooked the fish but now for once my salmon fishing experience came good. On 4 lb nylon and in heavy water much akin to a Scottish salmon river, my skill proved equal to the task of bringing this trout of almost seven pounds to the net albeit 150 yards downstream of where I had hooked it.

In very similar circumstances Jenny landed a six pounder and I followed with another of just over five pounds, each one fighting long and hard in the fast water. So far we had moved only about 200 yards upstream from where we had left the boat and were only too glad to rest gently after the excitement as Steve walked slowly up the bank looking for another fish. When he found it, Jenny, who by now was awake and really on the ball, had little difficulty in hooking and landing another brownie of just under 6 pounds. As we stopped for lunch we realised, to our amazement, that we had netted and returned four fish with a total weight of 24 pounds! We had fished for each one specifically and this was the moment when it suddenly came to me that there was something at least as entrancing as salmon fishing in Scotland!

Despite the fact that the wind was now getting up, the best was yet to come. Steve spotted a large fish under the far bank in a shallow but quite wide pool on a subsidiary stream and we crossed quietly below him and crept up on our knees to within about 20 ft of where he was gently weaving back and forth above a large piece of bank that had collapsed into the water, feeding below the surface. In the breeze it took me a far too many casts to get the fly even vaguely into the right place with a 15 ft leader, but eventually it landed just above and to one side of him, he turned slowly and deliberately, took the fly cleanly and, as he turned back to his original position, Steve yelled "strike" and he was on.

Despite his repeated efforts to get in under the high overhanging bank from which I had been casting, a ploy which we countered by re-crossing the river and pulling him out from the other side, he duly came to the net safely and turned the scales at just over 7 1/2 pounds. "You done really good there" Steve commented as he shook my hand - by the end of the week we had learnt that this was a really high accolade! If I had messed up that trout he would have had good reason to give us up as a bad job!

We next returned to the main river and in the middle of a fast run level with a backwater that made getting below it impossible, Steve put Jenny on to another large trout. For once there was no alternative but to approach this fish from above but the drag of the stream made the cast far harder than it looked and it took all Steve's considerable coaching skills before she got the fly in the right place. As seems so often to be the case in New Zealand, the trout took at the first good opportunity and, despite some weed placed between her and the main stream, Jenny soon landed the sixth and last fish of the day, a beautiful rainbow tipping the scales at just over 5 pounds.

The beauty of the South Island of New Zealand and the many and varied sights of interest that it offers, surely makes this a place that must be top of the list for any anglers looking for an alternative to our own overcrowded rivers. All you need is a guide - not cheap! - and a fishing licence which costs £9 for a week and gives you access to any river you care to fish! We were away for five weeks in all and the cost of the whole holiday including all food, accommodation and flights, campervan and car hire, excursions and helicopter trips etc. came to just a little more per head than one pays for a solitary week in Russia or Iceland!

*   *   *

Our efforts to catch anything at all in New Zealand without a guide were close to being farcical. On our first day there we went down to the river near where we were staying and managed a couple of small rainbows on a downstream "chuck it and chance it" basis and later on we caught three or four more similar trout while casting into the streamy water at the mouth of a feeder stream into a large lake. Beyond that our successes were nil but we did have one day when only the weather and our own total incompetence, we felt, stopped us hitting a high spot.

Gore is regarded as the capital of the brown trout world and, visiting the tackle shop there, we took advice from the proprietor who told us to go to a bridge on the main road a few miles out of the town, walk downstream and look carefully for anything rising in the long slow pool about fifty yards below the bridge. Following his advice to the letter we arrived to see monster trout rising everywhere. Now if you can see a rise you are in with a serious chance. The problem comes when you are fishing faster water and either the rising fish are impossible to see or, worse, they are feeding beneath the surface and only an experienced eye can detect them underwater. In this case everything was set fair for us. New Zealand trout are voracious feeders and relatively unfussy. If you stick to one of about three recognised patterns and present the fly with a small degree of skill you will probably lure the trout into taking the fly.

In this pool, with dimples appearing everywhere, Jenny took the first cast and immediately rose and hooked a fish of about 4 lbs. She was never at her best in the morning and it became a standing joke that she would miss the first three or four trout that came to her fly before she got into form. This was, however, the afternoon and her strike was perfect first time. However, things soon began to go wrong. After a couple of minutes the line went slack and, infuriated, she handed the rod to me. Collecting things together and getting ready to cast at another of the trout rising further up the pool, I became aware that the original one was still on! I handed the rod back to Jenny but, quickly though she tightened up on it and played it for a further minute or so, the damage had been done and it duly detached itself.

My own efforts were less good. I rose two trout and missed them both in quick succession after which things seemed to have gone off the boil and we moved downstream. It was a charming little river and we felt certain that we would catch fish. Then it started raining – heavily.

This had two results. In the first place the rises became almost impossible to see and in the second there were very few of them anyway. The trout seemed unwilling to continue feeding in the rain for the obvious reason that the fly had disappeared. So ended our nearly successful day.

*   *   *

I cannot wait to return to try again for these giants of New Zealand. My intention next time will be to have one week fishing with a guide in the North Island and another with Steve in the South and spend less time sight seeing. Hopefully New Zealand fishing will never get spoilt but the pressures are already mounting. Increasing numbers of foreign visitors are arriving each year and agricultural interests are pressing to extract more and more water from the rivers and streams to feed their huge irrigation systems. However, thinking in NZ is generally fairly straight and, hopefully, the powers that be will recognise the dangers early enough to preserve a wonderful wild commodity.

How one wishes that back home the government might find a tiny element of sympathy for the Atlantic salmon in its make up.

Quite apart from the fun we had fishing, we watched whales and endless dolphins, saw penguins waddling ashore to feed their young, took a helicopter up a glacier and visited the albatross sanctuary. If only I was thirty again I would seriously try and find a way of emigrating to a country I quickly fell in love with.

CHAPTER TWELVE

DEVON

As with Jenny's sailing so my idea that a move to Devon would provide me with massive opportunities for salmon fishing quickly proved misguided. This was not entirely due to the shortcomings of the county nor to any lack of kind invitations from the large circle of friends that we quickly built up. On the one hand I found that single days fishing were less than totally relaxing, while on the other the physical make-up of most of Devon's rivers proved to be less than ideal for odd visits at intervals of a month or so.

The main salmon rivers in Devon are the Taw, Torridge, Exe, Dart, Tavy, Teign and Tamar, the last of which, for most of its length. forms the boundary between Devon and Cornwall. Almost certainly I shall upset people who have fished all their lives on the smaller and less well known streams such as the Plym, Yealm, and Lyn, but, as I have no knowledge of them I cannot comment about them.

The Dart and the Tavy are almost spate rivers flowing straight off the granite hills of Dartmoor and providing, after rain, that wonderfully clear whisky coloured water that never goes really opaque. The Teign too flows straight off Dartmoor but seems generally to hold its level better than the other two. The remainder have to be counted as lowland rivers. Even the Taw and Exe, which rise on Dartmoor and Exmoor respectively, then flow through miles of farmland before reaching the best of their salmon beats. The Torridge and Tamar have no claim to moorland heredity. The result of all this is that after the rain, which all need so badly, only the Dart, Tavy and Teign are almost immediately fishable, while the Torridge and Tamar can take three or four days to clear adequately, by which time the level is already starting to drop and quickly reaches the point where more water is needed. Thus the "fishable time gap" is short and the occasional fisherman has to be lucky to get things right.

Further complications had to be confronted early in our life in Devon as our move west coincided with a really desperately bad time for the West Country rivers that entered the sea on the north coast of the County. The nets were taking huge numbers of fish and the rod and line anglers, to the despair of the riparian owners, were left with pickings that became more and more measly until, eventually, action was inevitable, painful, expensive and unsettling for all concerned.

It was against this background that we met yet another of salmon fishing's quiet and gentle men, Peter Norton-Smith. Peter has a distinguished war behind him in Bomber Command and is one of those unassuming people who tacitly earn one's respect without demanding it and, almost overnight, become the sort of friend whom one feels one has known for a lifetime. In addition Peter owns a lovely stretch of the Torridge at Little Warham near Beaford. This we were bidden, if not at will, at least when nobody else was on it, to go and fish whenever we wished.

It was sad that, as I have said, our introduction to this beautiful river took place just as its run of salmon reached its lowest ebb, but I nevertheless enjoyed a number of gorgeous and enjoyable days there, which yielded only one 3 lb sea trout and no salmon at all. The river has since returned to something nearer its former glory and I am delighted to say that "Trout and Salmon" has frequently, in more recent years, related both Peter and his wife Terry grassing a good number of fish. Our invitation still remains open and, though we have not taken it up for some years now, I hope that one day we may do so and perhaps be lucky enough to add a Torridge salmon to the few others that I have caught in Devon.

Peter has not been well recently but we did entice him to dinner a couple of years ago. At 84, he was comfortably the oldest guest but, in the same quiet way that I remembered from earlier years, he kept his neighbours at the dinner table engrossed with his stories and charm. From the other end of the table, I heard the lady on his right pontificating on a subject that she clearly knew far less about than he did. He let her ramble on for a few minutes and then, quite gently and politely, made it obvious in a few words that she was talking a lot of rubbish. After two largish gin and tonics before the meal, he put away his full quota of wine with it and was only too happy to down a brandy after it. When the time came for them to leave, I opened the door of his car for his wife to drive home, but it was he who climbed in behind the wheel. There cannot be too many of his sort left.

*   *   *

The Exe has already featured in the earlier pages of this book and seems to have suffered less than most other Devon rivers over the years, but it is not at all easy to get on to. Not being that close to it, I have never struggled too hard to obtain a rod on it, but for a year or two received an invitation to have the odd day on a beat between Exeter and Tiverton. This was at the behest of the then Vicar of Hatherleigh, Nick McKinnell, who, with his brother, owned a beautiful stretch near Thorverton. I only ever fished it in high summer and it looked lovely even then, but was not said to be particularly productive. The background to the ownership was interesting in that, at some time previously, a clause had been written in to a will stating that, in perpetuity, the beat could neither be sold nor let for profit. Neither Nick nor his brother had enough time, nor, most probably, the inclination to fish it very often and it has thus become a rather charming and wasted white elephant.

Once again I was lucky there. On a warm June afternoon in 1990 with the water dead low I suddenly found myself into a beautiful fresh fish of 8 lbs. If it was not very exciting, seeming to fight with a degree of the dilatoriness that goes with hot sunny days, it was certainly one of the most unexpected fish I have ever caught.

*   *   *

I have never fished the Tavy but am told that it is not very productive nowadays and therefore, although it is the closest of all to our home at Bridestowe, I have never bothered to put my name on the waiting list for a rod on the syndicate water near Tavistock.

The Tamar is likewise not far away and a lot of people, who have odd days on various beats on it have, in recent years, been kind enough to ask me to fish now and again. In addition, for a couple of years we took a beat at Lamerhooe for two days a month. Apart from one March day when we hooked and released three kelts in quick succession, we never touched a thing and eventually decided that we had better things to do.

I will doubtless displease a number of people when I say that I find it a rather unsatisfactory river to fish. Quite apart from the fact that it is almost always too dirty or too low to be in reasonable order, it is an oily green colour that I dislike. Beyond that I find it incredibly difficult to fish properly. This is certainly my fault, as my lack of ability to cast a long line results in my always finding that I cannot cover the best bits of the water in most pools. Those pools that have a good run of water into them at the head all seem to deepen unusually quickly after a few yards, making the wading difficult if not impossible and, constantly trying to reach that extra yard over an increasing width of slack water, is irritating at best and renders my fishing even worse than usual. It seems best to give the river a miss and I have now started to turn down invitations to fish it except, possibly, very late in the season.

In addition to all these problems the Tamar has the overriding disadvantage of having very few fish! This is a relatively recent downturn in its fortunes for I am told that in the '80's there were, in relative terms, plenty of salmon in it. There is now a small spring run, a few grilse struggle upstream in the summer if there is water and the main run of heavier autumn fish has been more and more disappointing in recent years.

The Dart is different in every way but one. It is easy to get day tickets to fish almost anywhere on it on Duchy of Cornwall water high up on Dartmoor. It is clear and never out of order even after a heavy flood. Such wading as is necessary in its higher reaches is generally relatively easy and one can pick and choose ones days according to the weather. Late in the season salmon can be expected in any of the beautiful though small pools upstream from Holne and a prolonged spell of wet weather in September will allow fresh fish to run up almost to the spawning grounds in a few days. Nevertheless, the head of fish is small and as yet, although I have only had a few late summer days on this beautiful river, I have never come across one. The many days of retirement that hopefully lie ahead of me will give me more opportunities and it remains one of my main aims to take a fish off Dartmoor.

*   *   *

The Teign is somewhat different. The best salmon stretches come well below the point at which it has run off the moor and it becomes rather treed, fairly heavily fished and regularly suffers from having spinners dumped into it. Day tickets for salmon are not impossible to obtain on the Upper Teign Angling Association water but, like all ticket waters, it is over fished when the water is right.

So we turn to the Taw. I had fished this river many years ago when I spent a week holidaying on my lonesome at the Fox and Hounds at Eggesford before I was married. We had no water, the river was dead low and a muddy grey green colour. In a couple of places distressed salmon could be seen lying in a few inches of water at the head of the pools trying to take advantage of what little oxygen the weak stream gave. I threw a minnow at a couple of them and they slowly sunk out of sight only to re-appear shortly afterwards in the same spot.

The Taw rises on Dartmoor and in the first mile of its considerable length is a crystal clear stream flowing down through Belstone and out into the Devon lowlands. By the time it reaches Eggesford it has been contaminated by miles of agricultural land and silt. Eventually it reaches the junction with the far cleaner Mole coming down from Exmoor through South Molton and from there on is a different and far lovelier river. More recently I have been invited to fish it quite regularly in company with yet another of fishing's seemingly endless succession of charming, quiet, elderly-ish gentlemen, whose family own a stretch about a mile long and including six or seven good pools.

Frank Pope was brought up in Crediton and tells stories of his father taking the train from there to the station at King's Nympton, fishing his way down to the bottom of the beat, having a little liquid refreshment at the Portsmouth Arms and returning by train to Crediton at the end of the day, often carrying several salmon.

Sadly those days have long gone. The train still runs but is now a characterless two coach diesel affair, while the river yields only a fraction of the number of fish it did before the war. Nevertheless it is as entrancing a river to fish as the Tamar is irritating. Every pool has a solid run into its head and then broadens and deepens to give a series of good lies that can be easily fished while the wading is, with one exception, simple and shingly.

For the majority of Frank's beat, which is now considerably shorter than it was in his father's day, a reasonable amount of water is essential but, at the bottom, one pool is best fished in low water. This makes it worth traipsing over there, a drive of fifty minutes across country, on a number of days when the greater part of the stretch will be too low and almost unfishable. The great problem, however, remains the fact that one needs water for it to be at its best, while after serious rain the river is too coloured to be fishable for two or three days.

There is an early spring run of heavy fish which go through these lower beats in March or April and these are followed by some large sea trout. When water allows, summer salmon come up from Barnstaple later on, together with a run of school peal. Normally by August the river is short of water and this state of affairs can last until the end of the season on 30th September. This results in a frustrating time for the anglers, who know that a fair number of fish are being held up at the mouth, where they are at the mercy of all the usual predators in the estuary. If there is good rain late in the season the Taw can still today be almost prolific. With his son, Anthony, Frank Pope had seven fish in a day a couple of seasons ago: almost unbelievable these days in the south of England.

This beat has provided me with a lot of entertainment and actually yielded the odd fish. In 2000 I had a big, red salmon in September which I put back. It looked to be about 14 lbs. Half a dozen casts later I hooked a smaller, fresher fish which I duly beached and knocked on the head. It was 8 lbs and only slightly less lovely than the proverbial bar of silver.

I fished with Frank for a day each week throughout the early part of last season (2002) but although fish had been reported in March, the river seemed strangely empty in April and May. In early June things changed for the better. Frank had a fresh run fish of about 7 lbs from a lie just above the top pool on the beat, and from a place that he had never in his long life fished before. Being unable to kill it, due the ridiculous laws that this country has adopted in recent years, I had to help him across the river to the only place in the pool where we could beach and release it. By the time we achieved this it had been hanging in the water for about ten minutes. Survival seemed unlikely and it was a waste of a good salmon.

Later on the same day I had a savage take in the heavy water of the bottom pool and it took me all of ten minutes to beach a sea liced fish of around 12 lbs. Again it had to go back. Up to 16th June when the law relaxes and salmon can again be killed, we fished mainly with single hooks to enable us to release them more easily. The result of this tends to be that sea trout, which, for reasons that nobody understands, can be killed at any time in the season, had a tendency to get off on the rare occasions when they were hooked. Nevertheless Frank did have a nice 6 pounder one day when he was with Anthony and a number of others were reported to have been lost. Since early July we have had no rain, the river is just a trickle and the drive to it not worthwhile. As I write this (originally on 26th August 2002) I am about to go north to the Farrar and just hope that when I get home in the middle of

September we will have had a few days rain and this charming beat will again be worth fishing.[1]

*　*　*

In essence and as far as I am concerned, that is salmon fishing in Devon. Twenty-three years of it summed up in just a few pages and a total catch of four fish and a small sea-trout – truly "Occasional Salmon".

---

[1] We didn't and it wasn't and the same happened in 2003!

CHAPTER THIRTEEN

RANDOM THOUGHTS

It always seems to me most strange that there are people in their twenties who publish some sort of autobiography. I wonder what they think they know about life at that age and why they feel that that is the right moment to go into print. How do they decide when they have reached some point at which they can publish a book when almost their whole adult life is before them?

In my case I have written this book not with the avowed intention or expectation of having it published, but rather because my memories keep jutting in and getting in the way of other things that I want to try to write. I cannot get on with the latter until the former has been dealt with. It so happens, however, that I find myself nearing the end of this book at a time that may prove to be some sort of watershed in my salmon fishing life. As I have written, the last thirty years of that part of my life has centred round two rivers, the Upper Oykel and the Farrar. Neither are, sadly, the rivers that they were. One hears dreadful stories of a dearth of fish in such wonderful rivers as the Dee and the Tay. The Atlantic salmon, one of nature's most miraculous creatures, is now an endangered species, beset by a myriad of problems. It seems impossible that it should disappear from our rivers and lochs, and yet one feels that the day when this magnificent fish will no more be seen struggling upstream at such places as the Falls of Shin, may not be so far away.

This decline has been going on for far longer than I can remember. Tales of enormous catches of huge salmon, from rivers all over the Kingdom at the end of the nineteenth and well into the twentieth century, abound. By then pollution had long since taken its toll of rivers such as the Tyne and Clyde, but the vast majority of Britain's salmon returned year after year, unrestrained except by their natural predators and by the estuary nets and the rod and line anglers. In the sixties, when catches were already a pale shadow of the past, the "disease" hit with a vengeance. Almost as soon as salmo salar was starting to recover from this catastrophe, salmon farming was a beginning to become viable. It took a little while for people to realise the dangers that this involved, but slowly its adverse effect on stocks of both salmon and, to an even greater extent, sea trout became obvious. Rivers and lochs in the west of Scotland were ruined and many businesses, built up over many decades and dependent upon the presence of these fish, went to the wall. Almost without people realising it, technology was about to strike at a whole industry.

As if that was not bad enough, as soon as the feeding grounds off Greenland were finally discovered, echo sounders allowed trawlers to detect shoals of fish in the deepest and most remote parts of the ocean as well as closer to home in the North Sea. The writing was on the wall.

Successive governments, both at home and abroad, have totally failed either to grasp the seriousness of the situation or to show any will to tackle it. Pressure groups here have had limited success in attracting adequate funds to enable them to highlight their case, but slowly the light began to dawn and the riparian owners started to look at their options and think about taking action.

Negotiations to buy off the estuary nets were never easy but in many cases were concluded with a considerable degree of success. Catches did start to improve in many of the worst hit rivers, particularly in England and Wales, and the awful records of the late seventies and early eighties on such rivers as the Torridge in Devon were slowly but steadily improved. In addition some rivers that had been terribly polluted throughout the time of the industrial revolution and on until well after the Second World War, started to be cleaned up. But neither of these two mammoth tasks could halt the countrywide, and even worldwide decline. Man's greed could not be restrained and the huge holds of enormous trawlers were increasingly filled with salmon to the benefit of a few and at the expense of a large part of the rod and line fishing industry.

Spate rivers had an additional problem to contend with. Acres of unattractive forestry were planted, with little thought for the future effect that the trees would have on the rivers and streams that they bordered. Rain that would previously have given a river almost a week of good fishable water, began to last for only two or three days before the height dropped again to summer levels. At the same time global warming started to kick in, resulting in shorter spells of heavier rain and longer periods of hot summer sunshine from the far south-west right up to the north of Scotland.

Anxieties steadily increased and the great and dangerous red herring of "catch and release" took hold.

When I was privileged to be asked to fish the Birse beat of the Dee for two days in May 1999, I landed a beautiful fresh run fish, which, on the prior instructions of the ghillie, I killed. I counted myself doubly lucky in that it was only the tenth of the season to come off this prime beat, where the feeling was that if fifty were taken for the season, they would have done extremely well this from a beat that used to boast a regular catch of three hundred salmon every season.

One fish per week per rod, however, was the rule and I was amazed to find that on fishing pool down again in the knowledge that, if I caught another fish, it would have to go back, I encountered a strange feeling of unreality. It was the first time in my life that I had cast knowing for certain that I was doing it for my own fun. The fish had indeed become just my toys. I did not like it!

Inevitably on one of the rivers most effected by the catch and release argument and where no concensus of opinion seems to exist, this subject was never far from anyone's lips. However the most generally held view on Royal Deeside can perhaps best be summed up by the following comment: "Obviously returning as many fish as possible can do no harm to the Dee and may help the position slightly. However, to suggest that this alone will make a massive difference is to mislead oneself and everyone else. Far, far more needs to be done if the Dee is to be saved". I believe more is now being done.

So many thousands of words have been written about the pros and cons of "catch and release" that the waters have become muddied to a point where the basics of the argument have become lost in the spate.

The two most extreme views are, on the one hand, that every salmon fisherman should release every salmon he hooks, regardless of every other factor, and on the other that no fish hooked and duly landed should necessarily be returned. Few will agree with either of these extreme views today, although it is as well to remember that it is a very short time since the latter was popularly accepted. But where ought we to draw the line of compromise?

I am old enough to feel that the solution ought to be very simple. It should be enough to apprise every angler of the situation faced by the river system on which he is to fish and, thereafter, to leave it to his intelligence and conscience to do what is right under the circumstances in which he finds himself. Sadly, very sadly, this may not be possible simply because we live in a world so imperfect that a few will cheat the system for their own ends! And yet, and yet...............! Hold on a moment! How many of those people are there, even today, fishing for salmon? What percentage of the total do they represent? And how much difference to the overall picture would it really make if they continued to dishonour such an unwritten code?

No field sportsman in the true sense of the word will put his head into the "catch and release" noose so far that he leaves himself open to attack by those who oppose game fishing. Their criticism of those who fish simply and only for the pleasure of hooking and playing a fish with no intention of killing and eating it, is very sound and very hard to argue against. (The natural extension of this, of course, renders every aspect of coarse fishing immediately indefensible but this must remain the concern of others!).

Likewise how many true field sportsmen, knowing the parlous state of the Atlantic salmon today, finding himself in a position to adversely affect the spawning situation of the river he is fishing, will actually do so. I suggest very, very few and, furthermore, we all know that very few will have that opportunity!

In 1995, as already related, my wife, my son and I were lucky enough to have a bonanza week on the Upper Oykel. Fishing two rods, we landed forty four fish between us, sent three to the smoker and brought fourteen south. The balance of twenty seven were returned. In the following three years the same week was blank simply because we had no water and in the following season it yielded just one fish despite two days of good water – and I returned that one as well. At that point we decided enough was enough. We knew we would pay a high price for the wonderful week in 1995 but did not expect it to be as high as that! The point I am making – and in fact repeating -is that while it may seem that to have killed seventeen fish in a week in 1995 was excessive, by the time we reached September 1999 the figure had become seventeen fish in five weeks. A bit different!

This year I was invited up to the Oykel again and, rather rudely, said I would love to come if there was water, but could not face a week sitting looking at the bones of the river again. There was a brief bit of rain giving reasonable water on the Monday, when we watched tens of fish, doubtless representing a true figure of hundreds, running for Loch Ailsh and not pausing to look at a fly. Quite by chance I did hook and beach one fish. It was a cock, it might have been over 10 lbs or just under and it was a bit red. Somewhat reluctantly I put it back. The rules of the river stated that all fish over 10 lbs, all hens and everything not fresh must be returned. Put another way, one was hoping to land a small, fresh cock and, frankly, I now feel it would have been more sensible and certainly less irritating to have killed that fish. The rule is surely flirting dangerously with the "toy"argument.

Similarly in England it is illegal to kill a salmon before mid June. On the Taw in Devon, it is possible to cast a fly before that with a clear conscience solely because it has a run of sea trout which can, for some unknown reason, legally be killed. Nevertheless I felt less than ecstatic when, as related in the previous chapter, my companion and I both had to return fresh run fish on 5th June this year, just nine days before the ban ended.

To put this whole question in its proper perspective I should add that I caught my first salmon in 1950 but only six years ago landed my hundredth. Hardly slaughter! It is not I and my sort at whom bag limits are aimed - rather is it aimed at those who are lucky enough to fish the best rivers at the best times for a number of weeks each year and who count their annual catch in the tens and twenties.

By definition those fishermen are the most likely to have regard for the future welfare of the Atlantic salmon, and thus will be those most likely to behave in a way that will accord with that welfare. If, amongst those lucky people, there exists the odd glutton, or, to put it more frankly, cad, then it will not be long before he is rooted out and sent packing.

Unless I am massively naive, we are not dealing here with a race that is either so unintelligent that they cannot see what the results of mass killing will be, nor with people who, living only for today, have to think of the next meal for their wife and family. We must, surely, give our fellow anglers credit for a modicum of common sense, and trust them to have some regard for the future of a way of life that they love. They will surely want their children to have the opportunity to enjoy salmon fishing as they have done and will thus do everything in their power to ensure that it is available in years to come.

So - let us, on the one hand, leave the whole matter of how many fish we kill to individual consciences, (he or she who has none will surely pay the price when he finally meets the fisher of men!). On the other hand let us start a determined and forthright movement amongst all salmon anglers to do more, much more, in other directions to protect the future of the sport.   One has to ask what percentage of salmon fishermen belong to one of the accredited salmon conservation organisations? What percentage of those letting rods by the day or week insist that their tenants or guests so belong? Do we know which of these bodies we ought to be joining? Have we any clear idea of the aims of each of them? Why is there more than one?

Next we should be asking ourselves what each of us is doing to add our pressure to that already being put on the government to tackle the root of the problem, which many of us are increasingly certain lies at sea, beyond the limit to which individual efforts can stretch. Which MPs or MSPs represent constituencies in which a salmon river exists? Are they doing enough, or indeed are they doing anything, to protect the welfare of that river? Does a list of them exist? Is it readily available? Where can it be found? By whom are they regularly hounded?

If we could find some way of preventing just one single act of rape against salmon on the high seas, would we not, at a stroke, be achieving more than do all the acts of catch and release in a whole season? A friend of mine fishing in Sutherland recently was bemoaning the apparent failure of the grilse run due, it was conjectured, to the extreme heat of the water in the river. Next day a trawler was said to have docked at Inverness, loaded to the gunwales with silver grilse scooped up from the coastal waters where they were trapped while they waited for the rains.

Is catch and release in fact not doing actual harm by drawing the attention of salmon anglers away from far more important matters? If the Atlantic salmon is to be saved for our grandchildren surely we need to look at far more radical methods than the returning of a relatively few fish, which might or might not survive, to continue their way to the redds?

In the past four years I have discussed the merits of "catch and release" with gillies on the Spey, Dee, Tay and Oykel. Not one of them believes that it makes a significant difference to the salmon stocks.

*   *   *

So it may be that this is a moment at which the direction of my occasional salmon fishing may change and thus provide a natural break which will give some point to the preceding chapters. After years of planning to return to such rivers as the Oykel or the Farrar in each succeeding year, I am, in this autumn of 2002, beginning to think about alternatives.

I may start looking at some of the slightly larger rivers, where shortage of water is neither so disastrous nor so prevalent. I may think about fishing abroad a little more. I may even see if I can get any satisfaction from catching a few trout.

*   *   *

At the beginning of this book I mentioned a hypothetical fisherman looking for the salmon fishing that would suit him best. I suggested that he asked himself amongst other things what was the most important moment in his fishing. After more than fifty years at the game it is a question that I still find hard to answer.

When I introduced my wife to fishing I said that most fishermen were charming people partly because it is such an uncompetitive sport. Uncompetitive? If you believe that you will believe anything. There may be people who catch so many fish that they care not a jot how other people fare: there may be some who take little notice of how many other people land from the same beat or the same river that they are fishing, but they are few and far between. A serious part of the pleasure most of us derive from salmon fishing, and it is best to admit it, comes from going back to wherever one is staying, be it hotel, lodge or private home, having caught a fish, landed it and having something to show for ones efforts. If this sounds unpleasant it is not really so: it stems from the quite natural feeling of wanting to show oneself to be other than a complete fool with a rod in one's hand. It is best if everyone has caught something, worst if everyone else has caught something and you have nothing, but perfectly acceptable if somebody else has a fish and others including yourself are blank. To that extent and quite naturally because a fish for the freezer is lovely, the actual landing of a fish gives one a great feeling. So, of course, do those superb moments while you are playing it, when it runs and the reel screams, or when you are faced with a problem such as a dead tree, to which the fish tries to run but which intention you prevent. Best, however, must be the actual second of the take and the short moments thereafter, when you begin to realise that it really is on and your contact appears sound. The thrill that runs through a salmon fisherman at such a moment exceeds any other sporting moment that I have ever known. Better than hitting a perfect half volley inches above the board in a rackets court, or bowling a perfectly pitched leg-break and taking the outside edge of a good batsman who is well set: better even than arriving breathless, but with the adrenalin pumping, at the end of a long run after a strong fox across Dartmoor.

*   *   *

I have tried throughout this book to avoid too much rather boring detail about the technicalities and niceties of salmon fishing, but must include a few pertinent comments to which some will doubtless take exception.

Having fished all my life with a single handed rod, and after taking into account the undoubted facts that the kind people who have invited me to fish, have gone out of their way to put me in places where great reach is not essential, and that I have generally chosen to fish smaller rivers rather than the great open spaces of the Tay or Spey, I can honestly say that I have only rarely found lack of length to be an overriding disadvantage. It is undeniable that a shorter rod will lead to greater care in the playing of big fish being essential, but, by contrast, the fun and feel of playing any salmon on a smaller rod is considerably greater than on a large one.

*   *   *

In the fifties single hooks were the norm. Beautifully dressed Silver Doctors, Green Highlanders, Blue Charms, Mar Lodges and a host of others bring back wonderful memories. It does not seem that their hold was any less sure than the treble hooked Ally's Shrimps or G.P.s of today. We never had more than one line. If it got too heavy and was sinking too much, you greased it so that for a time it floated. The golden rule was, as it today, to fish down and across and to cast more squarely as the water got slower. No great change of tactics there. Spinning was little more than a lottery unless an expert was in charge. The reels had strange brakes on them that were meant to stop the line overrunning as soon as the minnow or spoon hit the water. All too often the brake failed to work properly resulting in an infuriating tangled mass of lightweight silk line everywhere. Later the multiplier came in which improved things somewhat although overrunning was still something of a problem with them. Finally, it seemed almost overnight, the fixed spool reel appeared. Once the knack of using it had been achieved, it required little skill or knowledge to operate with reasonable accuracy and efficiency. It had a slipping clutch, which rendered the art of playing a fish virtually superfluous. Once the clutch was set at a level where the fish could take line if it pulled hard enough, all one had to do was to keep gently winding the line in. When the tension was stronger than the level at which the clutch was set, it slipped. Simply and with the minimum of skill the fish eventually arrived at one's feet. Quickly people who had never felt able to fish for salmon before found themselves, after a few practice casts on the lawn, able to set out with a realistic chance of success. Any idea that the satisfaction of catching a fish on a bait of whatever sort, equates in any way to catching one on a fly is a total misconception. The thrill of the long bending rod, the sound of the ratchet on the reel and the "feel" of the fish have all gone. It is a very second rate pastime and I have never understood why the practice has not been outlawed on rivers where spinning is presently allowed but "catch and release" in any form is operated.

Many fishermen turn up at the river with boxes and boxes of flies of all different colours, patterns and sizes. I do believe that colour is important but not always absolutely vital. Murray Harper, having landed eleven fish in two hours during our bonanza year on the Oykel, switched from orange to purple and the fish stopped taking, thus proving, at least to his own satisfaction, that salmon are not colour blind. Over the years I have taken fish from the same river on flies as divergent in colour as the Blue Charm and the G.P. but have recently come to favour something with a little yellow or orange in it. I have caught more fish on a Thunder and Lightning than on all other flies put together and strongly suspect that, if I had that fly in every size and a variety of dressing weights in my box, I would need no others.

*   *   *

A well known Scottish gillie recently said to me "We get lots of people fishing here in a season, but only a few fishermen". He went on to explain what he meant, but I already knew. With the coming of modern carbon rods, sinking tips, monofilament nylon and with "new" money spreading through the population, anyone can go out and buy expensive fishing tackle, go and have a few lessons, learn to cast overhead or roll cast or Spey cast in an hour or two, pay a King's ransom for a good beat and go and catch a salmon.

It takes longer, a great deal longer, to learn to read water, to play a fish well, to interpret the many things that make salmon fishing something just slightly more than a "chuck it and chance it" affair.

I have just begun, after fifty years at it, to think I know a tiny bit of the lore of salmon fishing. Catching fish is obviously the most important part of the whole game and a blank day or a blank week is never so good as one in which a fish is brought to the bank. To be able to enjoy a blank day despite its fishlessness is, however, not only possible but essential. I adore casting a fly down a perfect piece of water provided the slightest chance of a fish exists. I love the challenge presented by a stretch of water that needs to be read, where one has to say to oneself "I must try to hang the fly outside and above that rock" or where I have to slide the fly under an overhanging tree. I get as much pleasure in seeing a hind with a calf wading across the river in the sunlight fifty yards below me as I do from hooking a fish. Well, almost!

I accompanied my son one evening recently when he went down to the Earn in Perthshire to have a couple of hours fishing. He caught nothing but in that time we saw a swarm of odd cloured white bees, a flock of lapwings and an otter. We agreed that that was a pretty good exchange for a blank evening.

He has caught salmon and, if they are lucky, his children may, but I fear for the future of this most wonderful fish unless governments world wide wake up to the dangers that threaten it.

CHAPTER FOURTEEN

STOP PRESS

This short and simple book has been an unconscionable time coming to fruition. You will have found a number of dates quoted at which I was writing it but finally, in the spring of 2004, the time has come to make some decisions as to how to get it into print.

None of the things I have written need to be changed nor have any of my dogmatic views altered: in fact rather the reverse. However, the passage of more than two years since I first put pen to paper has resulted in a hardening of a number of my views and a change in my own and my wife's attitude and approach to a number of parts of our lives, including fishing.

It is inevitable that any country's politics will affect all walks of life within it and although the slide towards the desecration of the countryside has been going on for many years, the watershed of the 1997 General Election undoubtedly hastened this process indecently. There can have been few government actions better calculated to enrage country lovers than the appointment of Mrs. Beckett as supremo at DEFRA. Whether true or not, the impression that this woman has never worn a pair of wellies, let alone owned a pair, indicates just where she stands in the eyes of rural people. It was bad enough to have Mr. Brown, clearly himself out of his depth, trying vainly to deal with the foot and mouth outbreak: to replace him with someone whose only visible connection with rural affairs is that a large number of people think that she bears some resemblance to a horse, is an insult to the rural community.

It is pointless to pursue the hunting debate further. By the time this is in print another step may have been taken towards consigning the sport to the our memories, while the government turn blind eyes to the appalling suffering endured by equines transported long distances in dreadful conditions to end up on the dinner tables of our continental "friends".

The shooters are starting to glance around them with a degree of concern. Well may they do so as some aspects of their sport seem to many of us far more difficult to defend than hunting. With no knowledge of this sport I will refrain from being critical, although I can almost hear my wife in the background saying that this does not often stop me.

Few will be tempted to feel that fishing may be exempt from this sad downhill journey from realism towards the ignorant materialism that is the watchword of the early twenty-first century. Already the riparian rights of long term owners of many great fisheries in Scotland are under a threat that, while it may look veiled, is already causing tremendous concern. The poison of the salmon farms may be overstated but has certainly played some part in the disappearance of the West Coast sea-trout.

Out at sea, both in our coastal waters, to which foreigners now have fishing access over which our national government has no control, and on the feeding grounds in such far away places as Greenland, the salmon is monitored and hoovered up in quantities that make its future look unsustainable.

Years before Mr. Blair came to power this problem was swept aside, disregarded and scoffed at by both British and European governments. The benefits of the incredible clean-up of such rivers as the Tyne had gone a long way towards assisting the ultimate fate of the salmon. Following the dreadful years of decline in the sixties when UDN added its own death knell to the pollution of industrial areas like Tyneside, a start had been made on buying out the estuarial nets on a large number of rivers and catch and release had begun to make its appearance. The credit side of the balance sheet had a look of solidity to it.

Beneath the surface, however, insidious forces were at work. Global warming was leading to reduced overall rainfall and what rain was falling was tending to come in shorter and heavier spurts. The afforestation programmes of the late sixties and early seventies were starting to reveal themselves as the menace that they have now become, causing water to run off so fast into the rivers that a spate that would previously have given three or four days of good salmon fishing, now supports just one or two. But more threatening than this was a simple fact: fewer and fewer fish were returning to the rivers of the United Kingdom each year.

So what does the hypothetical fisherman in the first chapter of this book do? In most cases he learns to live with increasingly paltry returns for the investment he makes in his sport. He accepts unquestioningly that he will have to return most of the salmon he lands to preserve the stocks, his freezer remains empty of fish for longer and longer periods and he feels that wonderful moment when a salmon grabs his fly less and less often.

Some salmon anglers will travel less far, less often to have a blank week, thus restricting their chance of getting everything right even further. Some, like my wife and I, will look abroad. We shall shortly be leaving with a party of friends for the grilse run in Newfoundland[1]. We may return disappointed. We may catch as many fish as we are told to expect. Either way we will have fun, but that fun cannot replace the strange, almost romantic feeling of fishing in Scotland: the hot peat coloured bath at the end of a long, successful day casting into the same peat coloured water of a Highland stream, the purple heather covered banks and the constant presence of one's dogs. That really is life.

*   *   *

As another winter ends, hunting finishes and my thoughts turn again to trying to catch an occasional salmon, I can look back on almost fifty-five years of varied fortune in this respect, yearn for some parts of the past and hope there may be more good days to come. I cannot avoid, however, a feeling of gratitude that in 2004 I am not in my twenties or thirties.

I will end with a positive, if controversial, idea. I have long thought that nobody should be allowed to go hunting unless they can prove that they are members of the

---

[1] It was a disaster

Countryside Alliance, which, whether we like it or not is the only organisation trying to protect that sport. Many hunts find it impossible to insist on this for no good reason other than that they do not want to upset people.

Should we in the world of salmon fishing not accept that the future of the Atlantic salmon is under threat? If we do that should we not insist that everyone who leases salmon fishing in Great Britain, by the day, week or year, from a hotel, a club or a riparian owner is a member of one or other of the associations that are doing their best to protect the future of the salmon?

What we should be doing is to forget catch and release and initiate some system that will bring more money into those organisations that have the ability to act for the benefit of all salmon fisherman.

Yes, it would be difficult to achieve: yes, people would complain: but to paraphrase Burke "all that is necessary for the salmon to become extinct is for good men to do nothing".

ISBN 141202199-5

9 781412 021999